The BASIC Keto Cookbook For Beginners ON A BUDGET

by Martha Smith

Contents

Short History of the Keto diet

Keto nutrition is not new but has existed for a long time ago. It was created to cure people with epilepsy. In the 1920s, scientists discovered that elevated blood ketone levels will help patients to minimize their epileptic faints. Today the ketogenic diet is used to heal successfully kids with epilepsy.

Keto Diet?

The ketogenic diet is popular as a low carbohydrate diet which allows the body to produce small molecules of fuel called " ketones ". They are the alternative source of energy for your body when your blood sugar (glucose) is low.

Eating foods higher in carbs, your body is producing glucose and insulin.
Your body can convert glucose and use it as energy to be selected among many other sources.
Insulin helps to process glucose in the bloodstream, taking it around the body.

Ever since we use glucose as the main energy, fats are unnecessary and therefore stored.
By reducing the carbs, the body enters into ketosis.

What is Ketosis?

Ketosis is a metabolic process by which our body is supplied with energy from fats.

While we are in ketosis our body starts producing ketones, which are created by the liver from the breakdown of fats. The best way to get into ketosis is to follow precisely the Keto diet.

The liver then converts fat into ketones that enter the bloodstream and are used as fuel by the cells in the body, just like glucose. Providing energy to the body, ketones are the best fuel for the brain. If our brain does not reach glucose, we will not be alive.

But that does not mean that you need to get your glucose through food - the body can get the right amount of glucose even during prolonged hunger or a period of minimal intake of carbohydrates.

Getting into ketosis?

Here are the main signs that will show you that you are definitely in ketosis:

Increased urination- The keto diet is a natural diuretic so you will go to the toilet several times more than usual.

Dry mouth- Increased urination leads to dry mouth and increased thirst. Make sure you drink plenty of water and fill your body with electrolytes (salt, potassium, magnesium).

Bad breath -Acetone is a ketone body that partially releases in our breath. It can smell quite sharp, much like a nail polish remover. It is usually temporary and disappears in the long run.

Reduced hunger and increased energy - Usually, after going through the «keto flu», you will experience a much lower level of hunger and a «clear» or energized mental state.

You can test your ketone levels with blood sticks, blood meter or urine sticks. Also if you want to test the levels of acetone in your breath, you can use a breathing analyzer.

Keto Flu?

The first two weeks of your diet can be difficult and then you may experience what is known as "keto flu". Keto flu is your body's natural response as it adapts to burning fat for energy rather than sugar.

Symptoms include insomnia, dizziness, irritability, nausea, stomach pain, sore throat, cold chills, and muscle aches.

Keto flu usually lasts for several days, although symptoms can remain for up to a month. Whether you experience symptoms and their severity depends on your metabolic flexibility - the ability of your body to adapt to a new fuel source.

Metabolic flexibility is mainly determined by your genes and lifestyle. If you have been using a diet high in refined sugar and carbohydrates before you start keto, you will probably experience more severe symptoms.

The benefits of the Keto diet

Reduces inflammation: The Ketogenic diet is anti-inflammatory and can protect you from major degenerative diseases such as Alzheimer's and cancer.

Weight loss - Keto diet usually uses fat as a source of energy- so there are obvious benefits for weight loss. During a Keto diet, your insulin levels (fat hormone) are significantly reduced (your body is turned into a fat-burning machine). Recently, the ketogenic diet is showing better results than high-carbohydrate and low-fat diets;

Blood sugar control - The Ketogenic diet very easy lower the levels of blood sugar because of the type of food you eat. Studies have even shown that a keto diet is helpful to prevent diabetes. People who have type 2 diabetes, should be very careful with the Keto diet.

Focus and concentration - Many people use a ketogenic diet specifically for increased mental capacity. When you reduce your carbohydrate intake, you avoid large spikes in blood sugar. Together, all of this can improve your concentration and focus. Studies have shown that increased fatty acid intake can affect on our brain functions.

Increased energy - by giving your body a better and more reliable energy source, you will feel more energized throughout the day. Fat is the most effective molecule for burning as a fuel.

Epilepsy - The ketogenic diet has been used for the successful treatment of epilepsy. Today it is the best therapy for people who have uncontrolled epilepsy.

Cholesterol and Blood pressure - The ketogenic diet has been shown to improve triglyceride levels and cholesterol levels mainly related to plaque buildup in the arteries. In particular, other high-fat and low-carbohydrate diets show a dramatic increase in HDL and a decrease in LDL-particle concentration compared to low-fat diets.

Insulin resistance - Insulin resistance can lead to type II diabetes if not managed. Plenty of research shows that a low-carbohydrate ketogenic diet can help people lower their insulin levels to healthy limits.

Acne - Often, there is an improvement in skin appearance when you switch to a ketogenic diet. A recent study showed a decrease in skin inflammation when switching to a low carb diet.

What can I eat on Keto diet?

Fruits Lemon Raspberries, Lime, Coconut, Cranberries, Blackberries and Tomato

Veggies Kale, Cauliflower, Onions, Radishes Asparagus, Broccoli, Mushrooms, Cabbage, Aubergine, Brussel sprouts, Cucumber, Peppers, Artichokes, Pumpkin, Olives, Spinach, Green beans and Lettuce

Meat All sausages, Turkey, Chicken, Offal, Pork, Bacon, Lamb, Beef and Duck

Fish and seafood Snoek, Hake, Salmon, Calamari, Angel fish, Scallops, Trout, Tuna, Sardines, Yellowtall, Prawns, Scallops, Anchovies and Kob.

Eggs Organic eggs

Sauces and Condiments Tomato sauce, Hot sauce, Mustard, Vinegar and Mayonnaise.

Nuts Macadamia, Walnuts, Hazelnuts, Pecans, Brazils and Almonds

Fats Coconut milk, Lard, Duck fat, Mayonnaise, Coconut oil, Animal fats, Butter, Macadamia, Avocado oil, Coconut cream, Heavy cream and Extra virgin olive oil.

Herbs and spices Granules and Bouillon cubes.

Lunch & Deli Meats Salami, Prosciutto, Ham, Chorizo, Speck, Pastarmi, Bacon, Pepperoncino, Soppressata and Pancetta.

Dairy Feta cheese, Parmesan cheese, Cream, Butter, Greek yogurt, Cream cheese, Blue cheese and other high fat cheese.

Flour Hazelnut flour, Almond flour, Coconut flour and other nut flours.

What NOT to eat on a Keto diet

Fruits

All fruits & dried fruits

Alcohol

Thanks to the carbohydrate content, many alcoholic beverages can throw you out of ketosis, especially beer and liqueurs.

Starches

Starchy vegetables, soy, lentils, sago, tapioca, plantain, banana, and mesquite.

Flours

Wheat flour, cornmeal, arrowroot, cornstarch, cassava, dal, and fava beans.

Grains and grain-like seeds

Rice, wheat, quinoa, oats, amaranth, barley, buckwheat, corn, and millet.

Unhealthy Fats

Limit the intake of processed vegetable oils, sunflower oil and mayonnaise.

Sugars

Soft drinks, fruit juice, shakes, cake, ice cream and candies.

Processed vegetable oils and trans fats

Diglycerides, shortening, vegetable shortening, margarine, interesterified oils, corn oil, cottonseed oil, grapeseed oil, safflower oil, and soybean oil

Sauces

They often contain sugar and unhealthy fats.

Dietary and low-fat products:

Evaporated skim milk, low-fat yogurts, fat-free butter substitutes, and reduced fat cheese.

Tips for the Ketogenic diet

Here are a few tips, which will help you through your Keto adventure:

Minimize stress- when your stress hormones are low it will help you to enter ketosis

Sleep more- sleeping more hours will help you to burn more fat.

Choose your carbs very wisely-consume vegetables as a source of carbohydrates and like this, you will ensure your body all-important nutrients.

Exercise often- it will help your body to get into ketosis easily and will balance your blood sugar.

Stay hydrated- your body excretes more water on the Keto diet and you should increase your water intake.

Eat more salt- when starting a low carb diet the insulin levels are very low and you should increase your sodium intake.

Practice intermittent fasting- it will help you to get into ketosis faster.

Carefully track your carbs- be careful with Keto-friendly foods because they can be loaded with plenty of sugar. Always check the nutrition facts on each food you eat.

Use MCT Oil- help you to lose weight and support the good bacteria, which is good for the gut.

Necessary items you should have in your kitchen

Blender- you can use it for soups and smoothies

Tabletop Spiralizer- perfect for zoodles

Food scale- always keep a track of your portion

Electric pressure cooker- helps you to make the perfect Keto meal

Grater- great for cheese or some vegetables

Mixer- useful for dessert making

Cutting board- best option is to have two boards: one for veggies and another one for meat.

Rubber scrapper-good for stir, gather or scrapes food.

Measuring spoons and cups- important for the accurate measurement of your ingredients.

Most asked questions

Here are some of the most frequently asked questions about the Ketogenic diet:

1. How many pounds I will lose from the Ketogenic diet?
The effect will be different. Many people on the Keto diet will lose 1-2 pounds in the first week (mostly water). Thereafter, it is often removed about 500 grams of excess fat every week. After all, some will lose very quick and some slightly slower.

2. Can I monitor my carbohydrate intake?
Eat only the foods listed above in the list of allowed foods and you will not have to count carbohydrates.

3. What happens after reaching your goals (weight and health)?
Once you've reached your goals, you can either continue to follow the keto diet (to maintain the effect) or try adding a little more carbohydrates. In the second case, the effect of the keto diet will be slightly weaker and you can regain some of your previous weight.

If you completely revert to your old habits, you will slowly return to the weight and health status you had before. This is similar to training - if you stop doing it, you will slowly lose the benefits.

4. Will I be able to eat carbs again?
Of course. It is very significant to minimize the intake of carbs. After the first 3-4 months you can begin to eat carbs on special occasions - but go back to your diet right after.

5. Will I lose muscle mass?
Any diet is risky for losing muscle mass. But, consuming more proteins and the high level of ketones will help you to reduce muscle loss, particularly if you are lifting weights.

6. It is possible to build a muscle on a Keto diet?
You may gain muscle mass but it will not be the same result as a high carbohydrate diet.

7. How much protein should I eat?

The protein intake should be balanced, otherwise the high intake will increase the insulin levels and lower ketones.

8. Is ketosis dangerous?

Regularly ketosis is confused with ketoacidosis. Ketosis occurs naturally, while the ketoacidosis occurs only in uncontrolled diabetes.

Ketoacidosis is dangerous, but ketosis of a Ketogenic diet is completely normal and beneficial.

9. Is the keto diet safe for the kidneys?

Yes. So there is no reason to worry. Actually, the Keto diet can even protect your kidneys, especially if you have diabetes.

Sample Keto Food Plan for 20 days

To help you get started, here is a sample of a meal plan for 20 days

Day 1
Breakfast: Lemon Delights
Lunch: Veggie Finnish Salmon Soup
Dinner: Wrapped Chicken Bites with Bacon

Day 2
Breakfast: Colorful Sardines Omelet
Lunch: Family Salmon with Kale Pesto
Dinner: Fantastic Ground Pork with Broccoli

Day 3
Breakfast: Egg Muffins with Bacon
Lunch: Baked Codfish with Lemon
Dinner: Saucy Pork with Tomato Sauce

Day 4
Breakfast: Scrambled Eggs with Kale and Mozzarella
Lunch: Pork Steak with Spicy Asparagus
Dinner: The Best Chicken Legs with Parmesan

Day 5
Breakfast: Creamy Stuffed Spinach Eggs
Lunch: Bone- In Pork Chops with Brussel Sprouts
Dinner: Fried Salmon with Asparagus

Day 6
Breakfast: Delicious Keto Sandwiches
Lunch: Flavorful Beef Zoodles
Dinner: Easy Baked Tomatoes with Mozzarella

Day 7
Breakfast: Coconut Pudding
Lunch: Avocado Salad with Shrimp
Dinner: Mamma's Simple Roasted Turkey

Day 8
Breakfast: Blackberry Coconut Treat
Lunch: Quick Spinach Salad with Shrimps
Dinner: Beef Flank with Tomato-Pepper Sauce

Day 9
Breakfast: Stuffed Avocado with Egg
Lunch: Goat Cheese with Pecan
Dinner: Grilled Parmesan Pork Chops

Day 10
Breakfast: Cheddar Stuffed Zucchini
Lunch: Cauliflower Soup with Bacon
Dinner: Sunday Pork Burgers with Jalapeno

Day 11
Breakfast: Avocado Boats with Tuna Mayo
Lunch: Garden Zucchini Soup
Dinner: Teriyaki Shrimp Skewers

Day 12
Breakfast: Spinach Muffins with Parmesan
Lunch: Pan-Fried Monkfish Medallions with Lemon
Dinner: Winter Pork Soup

Day 13
Breakfast: Asparagus with Sauce "Hollandaise"
Lunch: Quick Beef with Broccoli
Dinner: Triple Cheese Stuffed Red Peppers

Day 14
Breakfast: Golden Cheese Crisps
Lunch: Sausage skillet with Zucchini
Dinner: Fried Sardines with Lemon Sauce

Day 15
Breakfast: Favorite Tiramisu Mousse
Lunch: Homemade Garlic Brussel Sprouts
Dinner: Greek Chicken Meatballs with Tzatziki

Day 16
Breakfast: Cocoa Smoothie
Lunch: Italian Melanzane with Parmesan and Mozzarella
Dinner: Pork Chops with Creamy Spinach Sauce

Day 17
Breakfast: Purple Raspberry Mousse
Lunch: Easy-Cheesy White Fish
Dinner: Beef Stir-Fry Delight with Cabbage

Day 18
Breakfast: Cauliflower Casserole with Cheddar
Lunch: Fresh Spinach with Tomato Sauce
Dinner: Marinated Pork Skewers with Mushrooms

Day 19
Breakfast: Grandma's Cheesy Omelet
Lunch: Italian Sushi with Prosciutto di Parma
Dinner: Dijon Chicken Breasts with Brussel Sprouts

Day 20
Breakfast: No-Bake Cheesecake in a Glass
Lunch: Summer Tomato Soup
Dinner: Marinated Beef Bites

VEGETABLES & SIDE DISHES

Low-Carb Cauliflower with Eggs

Ingredients

- 1 cup cauliflower florets
- 3 eggs
- ¼ teaspoon salt
- ¼ teaspoon pepper
- 1 scallion, chopped
- 1 tablespoon sesame oil
- 2 garlic cloves, chopped
- ½ teaspoon turmeric
- 1/2 tablespoon sesame seeds

Nutritional Information

292 Calories;
22g Fat;
4g Carbs;
1.8g Fiber;
15.5g Protein

Directions

Heat the sesame oil in a large skillet and saute the garlic for 1 minute or until fragrant.

Add the cauliflower florets and cook for 5 minutes or until it gets brown. Then crack the eggs into the skillet and add the chopped scallion. Stirring occasionally.

Season with salt, pepper, and turmeric. Cook until the eggs are set.

Serve sprinkled with sesame seeds.

Summer Tomato Soup

Ingredients

- 2 cloves garlic, finely sliced
- 1/2 large red onion, finely chopped
- 2 tablespoons olive oil
- salt and pepper, to taste
- 1 ½ tablespoon tomato paste
- 2 cups tomatoes, peeled and diced
- 2 celery stalks, peeled and chopped
- 2 cups vegetable broth
- 1/3 teaspoon paprika
- 1/3 teaspoon oregano
- ½ cup heavy cream
- ½ teaspoon dried basil
- ½ cup parmesan cheese, shredded

Nutritional Information

202 Calories;
16.1g Fat;
7g Carbs;
1.8g Fiber;
6g Protein

Directions

Heat the olive oil in a large pot, add the garlic, celery, and red onion. Cook for 2-3 minutes.

Then stir in the tomatoes, tomato paste, and vegetable broth. Season with salt, pepper, paprika, oregano, and basil. Boil for 20-25 minutes or until the tomatoes are soft.

Remove from the heat and blend with an immersion blender. Stir in the heavy cream and continue to boil for 1-2 minutes.

Serve in bowls and top with parmesan cheese.

Italian Sushi with Prosciutto di Parma

Ingredients

- 12 slices of Prosciutto di Parma
- ½ cups cream cheese
- ½ medium avocado
- 1/3 cup cucumber
- 1 ½ tablespoon sesame seeds

Nutritional Information

402 Calories;
44g Fat;
4g Carbs;
2.1g Fiber;
13g Protein

Directions

Lay the prosciutto slices on a flat surface. Then cut the avocado and cucumber into thin short strips with the same length as the width of the prosciutto slices. Set aside.

Spread a thin layer of cream cheese on each slice of the prosciutto. Place one avocado and one cucumber strip at one end of each prosciutto slice.

Roll up the prosciutto slices carefully and tightly. Sprinkle with sesame seeds and serve. Bon appetite!

Easy Green Baby Spinach Soup

(Ready in about 25 min | Servings 6)

Ingredients

- 5 cups spinach
- 2 small onions, finely chopped
- 2 medium-size carrots, finely chopped
- ½ cups coconut oil
- 2 garlic cloves, sliced
- 1 teaspoon pepper
- 1 teaspoon salt
- 12 cups water
- 1 cube vegetable broth
- ½ cup parmesan cheese, grated

Nutritional Information

173 Calories;
18g Fat;
3g Carbs;
1g Protein

Directions

Heat the coconut oil in a large pot. Add the onions, carrot and garlic. Sautee for 3 minutes.

Then add the water and the vegetable broth. Bring to a boil for 8 minutes.

Stir in the spinach and boil for another 12 minutes. Season with salt and pepper.

Transfer the soup to a blender and blend until smooth. Work in batches.

Serve hot and sprinkle with parmesan cheese. Enjoy!

Golden Cheese Crisps

Ingredients

- 1 cup Edam cheese
- 1 cup provolone cheese
- 1/3 teaspoon dried oregano
- 1/3 teaspoon dried rosemary
- ½ teaspoon garlic powder
- 1/3 teaspoon dried basil

Nutritional Information

296 Calories;
22.7g Fat;
1.8g Carbs;
0.1g Fiber;
22g Protein

Directions

Preheat your oven to 390F.

In a small bowl mix the dried oregano, rosemary, basil, and garlic powder. Set aside. Combine the Edam cheese and provolone cheese in another medium bowl.

Line a large baking dish with parchment paper, place tablespoon-sized stacks of the cheese mixture on the baking dish. Sprinkle with the dry seasonings mixture and bake for 6-7 minutes.

Let cool for a few minutes and enjoy.

Baked Green Beans with Parmesan

Ingredients

- 1 large egg
- salt and pepper, to taste
- 2 cups fresh green beans, washed and trimmed
- 1 teaspoon garlic powder
- ½ cup parmesan cheese, grated
- 2 tablespoons olive oil

Nutritional Information

207 Calories;
15.8g Fat;
6g Carbs;
2.5g Fiber;
8g Protein

Directions

Preheat the oven to 400F.

In a large bowl beat the egg and add the olive oil. Mix well.

In another bowl mix the garlic powder, parmesan cheese, salt and pepper to taste.

First toss the green beans in the egg mixture. Then coat them with the cheese mixture.

Place them on a greased baking dish and bake for around 13 minutes. Serve hot.

Stuffed Mushrooms with Bacon

(Ready in about 30 min | Servings 14)

Ingredients

- 4 tablespoons fresh chives, finely chopped
- 1 cup cream cheese
- salt and pepper to taste
- 1 cup bacon
- 1 ½ teaspoon paprika powder
- 14 large portobello mushrooms
- 3 tablespoons butter
- 2 tablespoons vegetable oil

Nutritional Information

176 Calories;
14.5g Fat;
6.7g Carbs;
3.3 Fiber;
7.5g Protein

Directions

Heat the vegetable oil in a large pan over medium heat. Fry the bacon until it gets crispy and reserve the bacon fat. Set aside.

Wipe the mushrooms and remove the stalks. Chop the mushroom stalks and sauté with butter in the bacon fat.

In a large bowl mix the fried bacon, sautéed stalks, paprika powder, cream cheese and chopped fresh chives. Season with salt and pepper to taste.

Spray a baking dish with nonstick cooking spray and preheat the oven to 350°F

Fill the mushroom caps with the mixture and arrange them in the baking dish.

Bake for 15 minutes or until golden brown. Bon appetite!

Homemade Garlic Brussel Sprouts

(Ready in about 40 min | Servings 4)

Ingredients

- 3 tablespoons olive oil
- 1 ½ tablespoon fresh chives, chopped
- 5 garlic cloves, sliced
- 2 cups Brussel sprouts, halved
- ½ teaspoon pepper
- ½ teaspoon salt
- 1 tablespoon fresh rosemary, chopped
- 1 lemon, cut in half

Nutritional Information

120 Calories;
7g Fat;
7g Carbs;
2.8g Fiber;
4.5g Protein

Directions

Preheat the oven to 350F.

Place the Brussel sprouts and sliced garlic on a baking sheet in a large baking dish. Drizzle with the olive oil.

Season with salt, pepper, fresh chives and fresh rosemary. Bake for 35 minutes and stir occasionally.

Squeeze the lemon over the top and serve warm.

Greek Cucumber Salad with Yogurt

Ingredients

- 1 ½ cup plain Greek yogurt
- 3 cucumbers, peeled and cut into small cubes
- 1 ½ tablespoon olive oil
- ½ teaspoon salt
- 2 tablespoons fresh dill, chopped
- 2 garlic cloves, minced
- 1/3 teaspoon ground pepper
- ¼ cup mint leaves, for garnish

Directions

In a large bowl combine the Greek yogurt, minced garlic, cucumber, and fresh dill. Mix well.

Drizzle with olive oil and season with salt and ground pepper.

Refrigerate for 30 minutes and serve with fresh mint leaves.

Nutritional Information

122 Calories;
6.2g Fat;
6g Carbs;
1.8g Fiber;
9.5g Protein

Cheddar Stuffed Zucchini

Ingredients

- 4 zucchini
- 1 cup tomato puree
- 2 cloves garlic, minced
- 1 small yellow onion, finely chopped
- 1 small red onion, finely chopped
- 1 large carrot, chopped
- ½ cup Cheddar Cheese, shredded
- 2 tablespoons canola oil
- 1 red pepper, diced
- ½ teaspoon oregano
- ½ teaspoon paprika
- fresh basil leaves, for garnish
- salt and pepper, to taste

Nutritional Information

204 Calories;
15.2g Fat;
6.3g Carbs;
2.8 Fiber;
6.3g Protein

Directions

Cut the zucchini into halves. Then using a spoon scoop out the flesh of the zucchini halves, but leave some at the bottom. Dice the zucchini flesh into small pieces. Set aside.

Season the zucchini with salt and pepper. Place the zucchini on a baking tray covered with a baking sheet.

In a medium skillet preheat the canola oil. Add the minced garlic, chopped carrot, diced zucchini flesh, diced red pepper, finely chopped yellow and red onion. Cook until soft.

Season with oregano, paprika, salt and pepper. Stir well. Then add the tomato sauce and cook for 7 minutes.

Fill the zucchini with the sauce and top with the shredded cheddar cheese. Bake for 20 minutes or until golden brown in a preheated oven at 400 degrees F.

Serve and garnish with fresh basil leaves. Enjoy!

Italian Melanzane with Parmesan and Mozzarella

(Ready in about 15 min | Servings 4)

Ingredients

- 1 cup fresh mozzarella, grated
- 1 large tomato, cut into circles
- 2 teaspoons fresh oregano, chopped
- 2 teaspoons fresh rosemary, chopped
- salt and pepper, to taste
- 1/3 cup vegetable oil
- 1 large eggplant
- ½ cup parmesan cheese, grated
- 1 large zucchini

Nutritional Information

297 Calories;
21g Fat;
7g Carbs;
3g Fiber;
14.7g Protein

Directions

Peel the eggplant and zucchini. Cut into circles and season with salt.

In a large frying pan preheat the vegetable oil.Fry the eggplant and zucchini until golden brown. Work in batches.

Preheat the oven to 400F and line a medium baking tray with parchment paper.

Place the eggplant circles on the parchment paper then add the zucchini circles and finally top with the tomato circles.

Season with salt, pepper, fresh oregano, and rosemary. Top with the grated parmesan and mozzarella cheese.

Bake for 10 minutes or until the cheese is melted. Serve immediately.

Ordinary Brussel Sprouts with Cheddar

(Ready in about 15 min | Servings 2)

Ingredients

- 2 tablespoons olive oil
- 12 Brussel sprouts, halved
- 3 tablespoons cheddar cheese, grated
- ½ teaspoon paprika
- 1/3 teaspoon salt
- 1/3 teaspoon pepper

Nutritional Information

288 Calories;
23.4g Fat;
7g Carbs;
4g Fiber;
10.8g Protein

Directions

Preheat the oven to 350F and line a large baking dish lined with parchment paper.

Place the Brussel sprouts on the parchment paper. Drizzle with the olive oil and season with salt, pepper, and paprika.

Bake the Brussel sprouts for 15 minutes or until crispy. Sprinkle with the shredded cheddar cheese and serve hot.

Roasted Peppers Salad with Feta Cheese

(Ready in about 15 min | Servings 5)

Ingredients

- 2 green bell peppers, roasted and peeled
- 2 red bell peppers, roasted and peeled
- 1 medium tomato, sliced
- 2 tablespoons olive oil
- 1 tablespoon balsamic vinegar
- 4 tablespoons feta cheese, crumbled
- 1 large red onion, chopped
- 1/3 cup kalamata olives, pitted
- ½ teaspoon salt
- 1/3 teaspoon pepper
- 2 teaspoons fresh oregano, chopped

Nutritional Information

380 Calories;
30g Fat;
7g Carbs;
1g Fiber;
18g Protein

Directions

Cut the roasted and peeled peppers into thin strips.

In a large bowl combine the sliced tomato, red onion, roasted bell peppers, and crumbled feta cheese.

Drizzle with the olive oil and balsamic vinegar. Season with salt, pepper, and fresh oregano.

Serve topped with the kalamata olives.

Cauliflower Soup with Bacon

(Ready in about 40 minutes | Servings 6)

Ingredients

- 1 medium head cauliflower, cut into florets
- 2 tablespoons olive oil
- 3 cups vegetable broth
- 1 onion, chopped
- 2 cloves garlic, minced
- 1/3 cup heavy cream
- salt and pepper, to taste
- 1 teaspoon dried oregano
- 1 teaspoon thyme
- 2 tablespoons butter
- 1/3 cup cooked bacon

Nutritional Information

151 Calories;
13g Fat;
5.4g Carbs;
1.5g Fiber;
2.4g Protein

Directions

Preheat your oven to 400 F.

Place the cauliflower, garlic and onion in a large baking tray covered with baking paper.

Drizzle with olive oil. Season with salt and pepper. Bake for 20 minutes in the preheated oven or until the cauliflower is fork-tender.

Place the cauliflower, onion and garlic in a soup pot. Add the butter, vegetable broth, oregano, thyme, salt and pepper. Stir well and boil for 15 minutes.

Let it cool for a few minutes and transfer the soup to a blender. Add the cream and blend until smooth. Work in batches.

Serve and garnish with the bacon. Bon appetite!

Fresh Spinach with Tomato Sauce

(Ready in about 20 min | Servings 6)

Ingredients

- 5 cups spinach, chopped
- 3 garlic cloves, diced
- salt and pepper, to taste
- 2 small onions, chopped
- 3 tablespoons butter
- 1 teaspoon dried oregano
- 1 teaspoon dried basil
- 1 cup tomato puree
- 1/3 cup water
- ½ cup goat cheese, crumbled
- 1 jalapeno pepper, chopped (optional)

Nutritional Information

292 Calories;
9.4g Fat;
6.1g Carbs;
2g Fiber;
4.8g Protein

Directions

Preheat a large saucepan on medium heat and add the butter.

Stir in the chopped onion and diced garlic. Saute for 1-2 minutes. Then add the water, tomato puree, dried basil, oregano, salt, and pepper to taste. Stir well.

Mix in the spinach and cook for 2 minutes more. Then add the crumbled goat cheese and cook for 1 minute more.

Top with the jalapeno pepper and serve.

Garden Zucchini Soup

Ingredients

- 4 medium zucchini, diced
- 1 large yellow onion, chopped
- 2 cloves garlic, sliced
- salt and pepper, to taste
- 2 tablespoons butter
- 4 cups vegetable broth
- 1 cup parmesan cheese, grated
- ½ teaspoon dried rosemary
- ½ teaspoon dried basil

Nutritional Information

154 Calories;
10.1g Fat;
6.8g Carbs;
0.8g Fiber;
6.9g Protein

Directions

Melt the butter in a large pot, saute the garlic and onion for 3 minutes. Then stir in the diced zucchini and cook for 8-9 minutes.

Add the vegetable broth and simmer for 12 minutes or until the zucchini gets soft. Remove from the heat and season with salt, pepper, dried basil, and rosemary.

Puree with an immersion blender until smooth. Serve hot and sprinkle with parmesan cheese.

POULTRY

Dijon Chicken Breasts with Brussel Sprouts

Ingredients

- 2 chicken breasts
- 1 cup Brussel sprouts, trimmed and halved
- 1/3 teaspoon salt
- 1/3 teaspoon pepper
- 2 tablespoons olive oil
- 1/3 cup balsamic vinegar
- For the marinade
- 1/3 cup soy sauce
- 1/3 cup olive oil
- 2 teaspoons paprika
- 1 ½ teaspoon pepper
- 1 teaspoon salt
- 1 ½ tablespoon Dijon mustard
- 2 tablespoons fresh parsley, finely chopped

Nutritional Information

580 Calories;
35.5g Fat;
6.9g Carbs;
1.8g Fiber;
52g Protein

Directions

In a large bowl whisk the soy sauce, olive oil, paprika, pepper, salt, Dijon mustard, and fresh parsley to make the marinade.

Add the chicken breasts in a large zip-top bag and pour in the marinade. Place in your refrigerator for 30 minutes.

Place the Brussel sprouts in a large baking dish lined with parchment paper. Then add the marinated chicken breasts to the baking dish with Brussel sprouts. Sprinkle with salt, pepper and olive oil.

Bake for 15 minutes in a preheated oven to 420°F. Serve immediately and drizzle with balsamic vinegar. Enjoy!

Bacon-Wrapped Chicken Bites

(Ready in about 20 min | Servings 6)

Ingredients

- 2 lbs. boneless chicken breasts, cut into 1-inch chunks
- 1 teaspoon smoked paprika
- 1/3 cup grated parmesan cheese (optional)
- salt and pepper, to taste
- 8 pieces of bacon, cut into thirds
- fresh parsley, for garnish

Nutritional Information

333 Calories;
13.2g Fat;
3.8g Carbs;
0.8g Fiber;
47g Protein

Directions

Place the chicken chunks in a bowl. Season with salt, pepper and smoked paprika. Combine well. Wrap the pieces of bacon over the chicken chunks and secure with a toothpick.

Preheat the oven to 350F. Then place the wrapped chicken bites in a large baking dish with parchment paper.

Bake for 15-20 minutes. Serve hot and sprinkle with grated parmesan cheese.

Greek Chicken Meatballs with Tzatziki

Ingredients

- 1 lb. ground chicken
- ½ teaspoon salt
- ½ teaspoon pepper
- 1/3 cup parmesan cheese, grated
- 1 medium egg
- 2 tablespoons olive oil
- 1/3 cup parsley, finely chopped
- 1/3 cup heavy cream

For the Tzatziki
- 1 cup Greek yogurt
- 1 tablespoon avocado oil
- 1 cup cucumber, grated
- 3 garlic cloves, minced
- ½ teaspoon salt
- 3 tablespoons sour cream
- 1 tablespoon fresh mint, chopped

Nutritional Information

354 Calories;
25.4g Fat;
3.5g Carbs;
0.4g Fiber;
27.7g Protein

Directions

In a large bowl add the ground chicken, pepper, parmesan cheese, salt, egg, finely chopped parsley, and heavy cream. Mix well.

Form into 15 balls and preheat the oven to 370F. Place the meatballs in a large baking tray covered with baking paper.

Bake for 16 minutes or until golden brown. Set aside. In a small bowl mix all the Tzatziki ingredients. Stir well.

Serve the chicken meatballs with the tzatziki sauce on the side.

Creamy Chicken Breasts

Ingredients

- 2 large halved chicken breasts
- 1 teaspoon salt
- 1 teaspoon pepper
- 3 cloves garlic, chopped
- 2 tablespoons olive oil
- 1 cup heavy whipping cream
- ½ cup parmesan cheese
- ½ cup chicken broth
- 1 teaspoon dried basil

Nutritional Information

486 Calories;
32g Fat;
4.7g Carbs;
0.3g Fiber;
43.6g Protein

Directions

Season the chicken breasts with salt and pepper.

In a large skillet on medium heat, add the olive oil. Cook the chicken for 5-6 minutes per side or until golden brown. Work in batches and set aside.

Add the chopped garlic, heavy whipped cream and chicken broth in the skillet. Stir well to combine.

Add the parmesan cheese and basil. Simmer for 4-5 minutes. Then return the chicken to the pan and simmer for another 1-2 minutes.

Serve warm and enjoy!

Non-Traditional Chicken Salad

Ingredients

- 2 chicken breasts halves, boneless
- 1/2 cup mayonnaise
- 1 tablespoon fresh parsley, chopped
- 1 scallion, finely chopped
- salt and pepper, to taste
- 2 pickles, chopped
- 1 tablespoon lemon juice
- 1 celery, finely chopped
- 3 tablespoons yogurt
- 1 tablespoon fresh thyme, chopped
- 2 tablespoons vegetable oil

Nutritional Information

324 Calories;
20.1g Fat;
5.6g Carbs;
1.8g Fiber;
29.6g Protein

Directions

Heat the vegetable oil in a large frying pan. Season the chicken breasts with salt and pepper.

Add the breast halves to the pan and cook for 4-5 minutes per side or until golden brown. Let it cool. When the chicken is cool enough slice into small pieces.

Add the chicken pieces, scallion, pickles, mayonnaise, and yogurt. Mix well. Stir in the fresh parsley, salt, pepper, lemon juice and fresh thyme.

Refrigerate for at least 30 minutes and serve. Enjoy!

Mamma's Simple Roasted Turkey

(Ready in about 3 hours| Servings 12)

Ingredients

- ½ cup soy sauce
- 1/3 cup fresh lemon juice
- 2 yellow onions, sliced
- 1 whole turkey (12-13 pounds)
- 1 celery, sliced
- 1/3 cup fresh rosemary, chopped
- 5 garlic cloves, sliced
- 1/3 cup fresh parsley, chopped
- 1 /3 cup fresh thyme, chopped
- ½ cup olive oil
- 2 cups vegetable broth
- salt and pepper, to taste
- 2 teaspoons paprika

Nutritional Information

450 Calories;
23.7g Fat;
4g Carbs;
4.3g Fiber;
56g Protein

Directions

Preheat the oven to 420F.

Pull out the giblets and remove the neck of the turkey. Wash the turkey and pat it dry with paper towels.

Place the turkey in a large baking dish. Put the celery, onion, garlic, fresh thyme, rosemary and parsley into the cavity of the turkey.

In a small bowl mix the soy sauce, lemon juice, olive oil, salt, pepper, and paprika.

Rub the mixture all over the turkey on the outside. Pour the vegetable broth into the baking dish.

Transfer the baking dish to the oven and bake for 2 hours and 30 minutes.

Then turn the turkey over and bake for 7-8 minutes or until the breasts get brown.

When the turkey is ready, transfer to a large plate and cover with aluminum foil.

Let it rest for 15 minutes and then carve. Bon appetite!

The Best Chicken Legs with Parmesan

(Ready in about 1 hour | Servings 6)

Ingredients

- 2 lbs. chicken legs
- 1/3 cup soy sauce
- 1/3 cup olive oil
- 2 teaspoons paprika
- 1 ½ teaspoon pepper
- 1 teaspoon salt
- 3-4 garlic cloves, minced
- 1/3 cup ketchup
- ½ cup grated parmesan (optional)

Nutritional Information

419 Calories;
22g Fat;
6.5g Carbs;
0.6g Fiber;
47.1g Protein

Directions

In a large bowl whisk the soy sauce, olive oil, paprika, pepper, salt, minced garlic and ketchup.

Add the chicken legs in a large zip-top bag and pour the marinade. Refrigerate the chicken legs for at least 30 minutes.

Bake the chicken legs for 20 minutes in a preheated oven at 350°F. Turn the chicken legs and bake for an additional 10 minutes or until they get tender.

Serve immediately and sprinkle with parmesan. Bon appetite!

Creamy Chicken with Fresh Asparagus

(Ready in about 15 minutes| Servings 2)

Ingredients

- 2 medium chicken breasts
- salt and pepper, to taste
- 2 tablespoons olive oil
- 1 lb fresh asparagus, trimmed and cut into 2-inch pieces
- 2 cloves garlic, sliced
- 2 teaspoons lemon juice
- 2 tablespoons butter
- ½ cup parmesan cheese, grated

Nutritional Information

506 Calories;
38g Fat;
6.8g Carbs;
2.3g Fiber;
46g Protein

Directions

Heat the olive oil in a medium pan. Season the chicken breasts with salt and pepper.

Fry the chicken breasts for 4-5 minutes per side or until golden brown and set aside.

In a medium skillet place the butter and the minced garlic. Cook for 30 sec.

Then add the fresh asparagus. Cook for 2-3 minutes or until the asparagus get tender.

Season with salt and pepper. Drizzle with the lemon juice and set aside.

Serve the chicken breasts and garnish with the asparagus and grated parmesan cheese.

Nutritious Chicken Stir-Fry with Cabbage

(Ready in about 25 minutes | Servings 2)

Ingredients

- 1/2 lb chicken breasts, boneless and cut into small pieces
- 2 tablespoons vegetable oil
- 1 yellow onion, chopped
- 2 cloves garlic, sliced
- 3 cups cabbage, shredded
- salt and pepper, to taste
- 1 teaspoon paprika
- 1 teaspoon lemon juice
- 1 teaspoon basil
- 1 cup vegetable broth
- 1 tablespoon fresh parsley, chopped

Nutritional Information

319 Calories;
18.1g Fat;
7g Carbs;
2.3g Fiber;
28,9g Protein

Directions

In a large saucepan, heat the vegetable oil over medium heat, then saute the garlic and onion for 1-2 minutes.

Then add the carrot and sliced chicken breasts to the pan and cook for 2-3 minutes.

Stir in the shredded cabbage and vegetable broth and mix well.Season with salt, pepper, paprika and basil.

Cook for 11-12 minutes or until the cabbage is tender.Drizzle with the lemon juice and stir.

Sprinkle with fresh parsley and serve hot.

Turkey Mayo Salad

(Ready in about 50 min | Servings 4)

Ingredients

- 2 medium cups roasted turkey breast, chopped
- salt and pepper, to taste
- 1 tablespoon lemon juice
- 1 cup mayonnaise
- 1 stalk celery, chopped
- 1 tablespoon Dijon mustard
- 2 tablespoons greek yogurt
- 1 teaspoon fresh basil
- 1 teaspoon fresh parsley
- 1 tablespoon olive oil

Nutritional Information

492 Calories;
29g Fat;
3.7g Carbs;
1.2g Fiber;
46g Protein

Directions

In a large bowl mix the chopped roasted turkey, celery, basil and parsley.

In a medium bowl mix the mayonnaise, lemon juice, Dijon mustard, greek yogurt, olive oil, salt and pepper. Stir.

Add the mayo mixture to the turkey mixture. Combine well. Place in the refrigerator for 40 minutes or more.

Serve on a bed of lettuce or with avocado slices (optional). Bon appetite!

Chicken with Green Beans

(Ready in about 30 minutes | Servings 2)

Ingredients

- ½ lb chicken breasts, boneless and skinless
- 3 cups fresh green beans, rinsed and trimmed
- 1 teaspoon onion powder
- 2 scallions, chopped
- salt and pepper, to taste
- 2 cloves garlic, minced
- 2 tablespoons vegetable oil
- 3 tablespoons vegetable broth
- 1 teaspoon red pepper flakes

Nutritional Information

370 Calories;
24.1g Fat;
6.2g Carbs;
3.3g Fiber;
27g Protein

Directions

Cut the chicken breasts into cubes and season them with salt, pepper, red pepper flakes and onion powder.

Heat 1 tablespoon of the vegetable oil in a medium frying pan over medium heat.

Place the chicken cubes to the pan and fry for 5-6 minutes or until golden brown. Stir occasionally and set aside.

In the same skillet add the remaining vegetable oil.

Stir in the garlic and green beans. Saute for 2 minutes and add the chopped scallions and vegetable broth.

Season with salt and pepper. Cook until the green beans get tender.

Serve the chicken cubes topped with the green beans.

Crunchy Fried Chicken Bites

(Ready in about 15 minutes| Servings 6)

Ingredients

- 1 ½ lb chicken breast, cut into cubes
- 1 teaspoon Kosher salt
- 1 teaspoon pepper
- 2 teaspoons rosemary
- 1/3 cup vegetable oil
- 3 small eggs
- 1 cup almond flour
- 2 teaspoons paprika
- 1 teaspoon garlic powder
- ½ cup parmesan cheese, grated

Nutritional Information

368 Calories;
25.4g Fat;
2.6g Carbs;
0.3g Fiber;
28.9g Protein

Directions

In a large bowl beat the eggs. In another bowl add the almond flour, paprika, garlic powder, salt, pepper, and rosemary. Mix.

First, dip the chicken cubes into the egg mixture and then into the dry mix. Coat well and work in batches.

Heat the olive oil in a large pot over medium heat. Transfer the chicken cubes into the pot and fry for 3-4 minutes or until brown.

Serve hot and sprinkle with parmesan cheese.

Chicken Fillet with Tomato Sauce

(Ready in about 25 min | Servings 4)

Ingredients

- 3 tablespoons olive oil
- 1 teaspoon salt
- 1 teaspoon pepper
- 3 cloves garlic, minced
- 2 tablespoons butter
- 1 red onion, chopped
- 3 cups plum tomatoes, diced
- ½ teaspoon dried basil
- 2 chicken breast halves, boneless and skinless
- ½ teaspoon oregano
- 3 tablespoons tomato paste
- 1/3 cup fresh parsley (optional)

Nutritional Information

448 Calories;
27.2g Fat;
5.6g Carbs;
2.1g Fiber;
42.6g Protein

Directions

In a large skillet preheat the olive oil.

Season the chicken breasts with salt, pepper, basil and oregano. Add the chicken breasts to the skillet and cook 5-6 minutes per side or until golden brown. Work in batches and set aside.

In the same skillet add the butter, minced garlic and chopped red onion. Saute 1-2 minutes and then add the diced tomatoes and tomato paste. Simmer for 5-6 minutes.

Place the chicken breasts back to the skillet and cook for another 2-3 minutes with the tomato sauce.

Serve warm and sprinkle with fresh parsley

Roasted Chicken Breast with Garlic Sauce

Ingredients

- 2 tablespoons onion powder
- 1 teaspoon Kosher salt
- 1 teaspoon dried oregano
- 1 teaspoon pepper
- 2 boneless chicken breasts
- 1 tablespoon garlic powder
- 3 tablespoons olive oil
- 2 teaspoons rosemary
- 1 tablespoon fresh parsley, chopped

For the garlic sauce
- 1 teaspoon dried thyme
- 1/3 cup fresh lemon juice
- 3 tablespoons melted butter
- 1 cup vegetable broth
- 12 garlic cloves, peeled and chopped
- ½ tablespoon coconut flour
- 1 teaspoon dried rosemary
- 1 tablespoon fresh parsley, chopped
- salt and pepper to taste
- ½ tablespoon dried sage leaves

Nutritional Information

450 Calories;
24.3g Fat;
5.2g Carbs;
0.3g Fiber;
47.9g Protein

Directions

Preheat the oven to 430°F.

In a small bowl combine the dried oregano, garlic powder, kosher salt, pepper, onion powder, olive oil and rosemary. Mix well.

Rub the mixture onto the chicken breasts. Place the chicken breasts in a medium roasting pan and pour over the lemon juice.

Bake for 15 minutes or until it is cooked through. Transfer the chicken to a plate and cover with foil. Leave to rest for 10 minutes.

In a medium saucepan add the melted butter and the coconut flour. Stir constantly for 2 minutes.

Add the dried thyme, garlic, vegetable broth, rosemary, sage leaves, parsley, salt and pepper to taste. Mix well and cook until it gets thick.

Serve the chicken with the garlic sauce and sprinkle with parsley.

Mediterranean Chicken with Yogurt Dip

(Ready in about 60 minutes| Servings 4)

Ingredients

- 4 chicken breasts
- 4 tablespoons olive oil
- 1 teaspoon dried thyme
- 3 cloves garlic, chopped
- 1 ½ teaspoon dried oregano
- 1/3 cup balsamic vinegar
- 2 teaspoons dried rosemary
- 1 cup fresh chopped parsley
- salt and pepper, to taste

For the Yogurt sauce
- 1 ½ cup greek yogurt
- 1 tablespoon lemon juice
- 1 ½ teaspoon garlic powder
- 2 tablespoons fresh dill, chopped
- salt and pepper, to taste
- 1 tablespoon olive oil

Nutritional Information

427 Calories;
28g Fat;
5.1g Carbs;
2g Fiber;
30g Protein

Directions

In a large bowl, mix the garlic, olive oil, balsamic vinegar, thyme, oregano, rosemary, and parsley. Add salt and pepper.

Place the chicken into the bowl and marinate in the refrigerator for 40 minutes.

Meanwhile preheat the grill to medium.

Place the chicken and grill for 4-5 minutes on each side until golden brown. Set aside.

In a medium bowl add the yogurt, fresh dill, olive oil, garlic powder, lemon juice, salt, and pepper. Mix well.

Serve the chicken breasts garnished with the yogurt sauce.

Warm Chicken Soup

(Ready in about 30 minutes| Servings 6)

Ingredients

- 1 ½ lb grilled chicken breasts, shredded
- 7 cups vegetable broth
- 2 garlic cloves, diced
- 1 yellow onion, diced
- ½ teaspoon paprika
- 1 bay leaf
- ½ cup celery, diced
- 1 medium carrot diced
- 2 tablespoons avocado oil
- 2 cups cauliflower
- 2 tablespoons fresh cilantro, chopped
- ¼ teaspoon salt
- 1 teaspoon dried rosemary
- ¼ teaspoon pepper
- 2 tablespoons fresh parsley

Directions

Heat the avocado oil in a large pot over medium heat. Saute the garlic for 1 minute. Then add the onion and carrot. Cook for 2-3 minutes.

Stir in the vegetable broth and celery. Boil for 8-9 minutes. Season with salt, pepper, rosemary, paprika, fresh cilantro, and bay leaf.

Then add the shredded chicken and cauliflower. Simmer for another 11 minutes.

Serve immediately and sprinkle with fresh parsley.

Nutritional Information

260 Calories;
8.3g Fat;
4.2g Carbs;
1.3g Fiber;
36.2g Protein

PORK

Creamy Pork Loin Steaks with Spinach Sauce

Ingredients

- 2 pork loin steaks
- 2 tablespoons vegetable oil
- 1 teaspoon pepper
- 1/2 cup cream cheese
- 3 tablespoons vegetable broth
- 2 garlic cloves, minced
- 2 cups fresh spinach, washed and chopped
- 1 teaspoon Kosher salt
- 1 teaspoon dried rosemary

Nutritional Information

332 Calories;
15.3g Fat;
3.2g Carbs;
1.1g Fiber;
43.2g Protein

Directions

Heat 1 tablespoon of the vegetable oil in a preheated on medium heat pan.

Season the pork loin with salt and pepper. Add the pork loin to the pan and cook for 4-5 minutes per side or until browned. Set aside.

In a medium saucepan add the remaining vegetable oil and garlic. Fry the garlic for 1 minute and add the spinach.

Cook the spinach until it gets wilted and stir in the cream cheese and vegetable broth. Season with Kosher salt, pepper, and dried rosemary.

Simmer for 5-6 minutes or until the sauce gets thick. Serve the pork loin topped with the spinach sauce.

Best Pork Sirloin with Bell Peppers

Ingredients

- 2 lbs pork sirloin steak, cut into cubes
- salt and pepper, to taste
- 4 large red peppers, sliced
- 2 cloves garlic, minced
- 2 tablespoons vegetable oil
- 1/2 cup vegetable broth
- 2 teaspoons fresh thyme
- 2 teaspoons fresh parsley
- 2 tablespoons butter

Nutritional Information

460 Calories;
30.1g Fat;
5g Carbs;
1g Fiber;
41.4g Protein

Directions

Heat the vegetable oil in a large skillet over medium heat. Season the pork cubes with salt and pepper.

Place the pork sirloin to the skillet and cook for 3 minutes per side or until golden brown. Transfer to a plate and set aside.

In another skillet melt the butter and saute the garlic until fragrant. Add the peppers and fry for 3 minutes. Then add the vegetable broth and simmer until the sauce gets thick.

Return the pork sirloin to the skillet and cook for 1 minute more. Sprinkle with fresh thyme and parsley, then serve.

Juicy Pork Chops with Mushrooms

(Ready in about 25 minutes| Servings 2)

Ingredients

- 2 pork chops, boneless
- 2 tablespoons vegetable oil
- 2 tablespoons butter
- 1 yellow onion, sliced
- 2 cloves garlic, minced
- 1 cup vegetable broth
- salt and pepper, to taste
- ½ teaspoon paprika
- 1 cup mushrooms, cut into ½ inch pieces
- 1 tablespoon fresh parsley, chopped

Nutritional Information

512 Calories;
35g Fat;
4g Carbs;
0.8g Fiber;
42.1g Protein

Directions

Heat the vegetable oil in a large pan over high heat. Season the pork chops with paprika, salt and pepper.

Place the pork chops in the pan and fry for 3-4 minutes per side or until golden brown. Remove from the pan and set aside.

In a large skillet add the butter, minced garlic, mushrooms and diced onion. Saute for 3-4 minutes. Season with salt and pepper. Cook until golden brown.

Pour in the vegetable broth and simmer for 5-6 minutes or until the sauce gets thick.

Place the pork chops to the skillet and cook for 1 minute more. Sprinkle with fresh parsley and serve immediately.

Bone-In Pork Chops with Brussels Sprouts

(Ready in about 30 min | Servings 4)

Ingredients

- 2 bone-in pork chops
- 1 teaspoon salt
- 1 teaspoon pepper
- 2 tablespoons vegetable oil
- 2 cloves garlic, minced
- 1 teaspoon dried rosemary
- 2 cups Brussels sprouts, trimmed and halved
- 2 tablespoons mustard

Nutritional Information

480 Calories;
16.2g Fat;
6.9g Carbs;
2.9g Fiber;
29.6g Protein

Directions

Preheat the oven to 300F.

In a large bowl combine the Brussel sprouts with the salt, pepper, dried rosemary, minced garlic, honey, mustard and one tablespoon vegetable oil.

Spread on the Brussel sprouts on a cooking sheet in a large baking tray. Bake for 20 minutes or until golden brown. Set aside.

Season the pork chops with salt and pepper. In a large skillet heat the remaining vegetable oil. Add the pork chops and cook for 4-5 minutes per side or until browned.

Serve the pork chops with the Brussel sprouts on the side. Bon appetite!

Friday Pork Skewers with Mushrooms

(Ready in about 1 hour 20 minutes| Servings 6)

Ingredients

- 2 tablespoons olive oil
- 1 teaspoon turmeric
- 2 tablespoons soy sauce
- 4 mushrooms, cut into quarters
- 2 tablespoons honey
- 1 ½ lb boneless pork loin, cut into cubes
- 1 teaspoon red pepper flakes
- 2 tablespoons with lemon juice
- 4 mushrooms, cut into quarters
- 1 teaspoon salt

Nutritional Information

275 Calories;
11.4g Fat;
6g Carbs;
0.6g Fiber;
33.1g Protein

Directions

Place the soy sauce, turmeric, lemon juice, salt, honey, red pepper flakes and olive oil in a large bowl. Whisk well.

Add the pork cubes to the bowl. Stir well. Cover with plastic wrap. Refrigerate for 1 hour.

Soak the wooden skewers in water for 30 minutes and preheat the grill on medium heat.

Thread the pork cubes and mushrooms onto the skewers.

Grill for 4- 5 minutes on each side or until it is cooked. Serve hot!

Sunday Pork Burgers with Jalapeno

Ingredients

- 1/2 lb ground pork
- 1 tablespoon onion powder
- 2 tablespoons fresh oregano, finely chopped
- ½ teaspoon salt
- ½ teaspoon dried basil
- ½ teaspoon pepper
- 3 tablespoons vegetable oil

For the topping
- 4 tablespoons mayonnaise
- 4 lettuce leaves
- 1 large red onion, sliced
- 4 strips bacon,
- 1 jalapeno, chopped

Directions

In a medium bowl mix the ground pork, onion powder, oregano, basil, salt, and pepper. Combine well.

Shape the burgers with wet hands and apply the vegetable oil on the meat. Grill for 6-7 minutes or until it is done.

Serve on lettuce leaves topped with onion, bacon, mayonnaise and chopped jalapeno pepper.

Nutritional Information

461 Calories;
37.5g Fat;
6.8g Carbs;
2g Fiber;
23.5g Protein

Mamma's Meatballs with Yogurt Sauce

Ingredients

- 1 lb. pork mince
- ½ teaspoon salt
- ½ teaspoon pepper
- 1/3 cup parmesan cheese, grated
- 1 medium egg
- 2 tablespoons olive oil
- 1/3 cup parsley, finely chopped
- 1/3 cup heavy cream

For the Yoghurt sauce

- ½ cup Greek-style yogurt
- 1 tablespoon olive oil
- 2 garlic cloves, minced
- ½ teaspoon salt
- 1 tablespoon fresh dill, chopped

Nutritional Information

421 Calories;
31g Fat;
4.1g Carbs;
0.5g Fiber;
28.6g Protein

Directions

Preheat the oven to 350F.

In a large bowl mix the pork mince, salt, pepper, parmesan cheese, egg, finely chopped parsley and heavy cream. Mix well. Form the mixture into 15 balls.

Place the meatballs in a large baking tray covered with baking paper. Bake for 6-7 minutes per side or until golden brown. Set aside.

In a small bowl mix the greek yogurt, olive oil, minced garlic, salt and chopped dill. Stir well.

Serve the meatballs with the yogurt sauce on the side.

Colorful Pork Salad

Ingredients

- ½ lb pork tenderloin, cut into thin strips
- 2 small tomatoes, chopped
- ½ cup Swiss cheese, cubed
- 1 red bell pepper, cut into strips
- 1 small cucumber, sliced
- ½ package fresh spinach
- 1 stalk celery, chopped
- 2 tablespoons vegetable oil

For the dressing
- 2 tablespoons balsamic vinegar
- ½ teaspoon salt
- 1 tablespoon Dijon mustard
- 2 tablespoons olive oil
- 1/3 teaspoon pepper

Nutritional Information

440 Calories;
27.2g Fat;
7g Carbs;
3g Fiber;
42g Protein

Directions

Heat a medium frying pan over medium heat.

Add the vegetable oil and pork strips. Fry them 1-2 minutes per side and set aside.

In a small bowl add the balsamic vinegar, salt, olive oil, pepper and Dijon mustard. Combine well.

In a large bowl mix the tomatoes, red bell pepper, cucumber, fresh spinach, celery, cubed Swiss cheese and pork strips. Drizzle with the dressing and stir.

Serve immediately. Bon appetite!

Winter Pork Soup

(Ready in about 20 minutes| Servings 3)

Ingredients

- 1 ½ cup pulled pork, cooked and shredded
- 4 cups vegetable broth
- 2 garlic cloves, diced
- 1 yellow onion, diced
- ½ teaspoon paprika
- ½ teaspoon cumin
- ¼ teaspoon salt
- ¼ teaspoon pepper
- ½ cup celery, diced
- 1 large carrot diced
- 2 tablespoons vegetable oil
- 1 cup baby spinach
- 2 tablespoons fresh cilantro, chopped

Directions

Heat the vegetable oil in a large pot. Saute the garlic for 1 minute and then add the onion. Cook for 2-3 minutes.

Stir in the vegetable broth, carrot, celery, baby spinach and pulled pork.Season with salt, pepper, cumin and paprika.

Boil for 15 minutes. Serve hot and sprinkle with fresh cilantro.

Nutritional Information

225 Calories;
13.1g Fat;
6g Carbs;
1.1g Fiber;
18g Protein

Grilled Parmesan Pork Chops

(Ready in about 25 min | Servings 2)

Ingredients

- 2 pork chops
- 1 teaspoon oregano
- 1 teaspoon onion powder
- 1/3 teaspoon chili powder
- 1 ½ tablespoon avocado oil
- 1/3 cup parmesan cheese, grated
- 1 teaspoon garlic powder
- 1 ½ tablespoons dried parsley
- ½ teaspoon dried thyme
- ½ teaspoon paprika
- salt and pepper, to taste
- 3 tablespoons fresh cilantro
- 1/2 tablespoon sesame seeds

Nutritional Information

526 Calories;
33g Fat;
5.8g Carbs;
1.5g Fiber;
46g Protein

Directions

Season the pork chops with salt and pepper.

In a large bowl mix the avocado oil, parmesan, oregano, onion powder, chili powder, garlic powder, dried parsley, thyme and paprika. Soak the pork chops in the bowl for 15 minutes and refrigerate.

Preheat a grill pan to medium-high. Grill until golden brown, around 4-5 minutes per side.

Serve with fresh cilantro and sprinkle with sesame seeds. Bon appetite!

Fantastic Ground Pork with Broccoli

(Ready in about 20 minutes | Servings 4)

Ingredients

- ½ cup butter
- 5 cups broccoli florets
- 1 lb ground pork
- salt and pepper, to taste
- 1 yellow onion, chopped
- 2 garlic cloves, minced
- ½ teaspoon dried thyme
- 1 tablespoon fresh parsley, chopped
- 2 tablespoons sesame oil

Nutritional Information

641 Calories;
55.1 Fat;
4g Carbs;
2g Fiber;
32g Protein

Directions

In a large skillet heat the sesame oil.

Add the ground pork and season with salt, pepper, and thyme. Cook for 7-8 minutes or until it is cooked through. Set aside.

In a medium pan heat up the butter and add the minced garlic, cook for 1 minute.

Stir in the broccoli florets, chopped onion and continue cooking for 5-6 minutes. Season with salt, pepper and fresh parsley.

Serve the ground pork warm and garnish with the broccoli.

Fancy Pork Medallions with Cheese Sauce

(Ready in about 10 minutes | Servings 2)

Ingredients

- 1/2 lb pork loin
- 1 teaspoon salt
- 2 tablespoons vegetable oil
- 1 teaspoon pepper
- 2 cloves garlic, chopped
- 2 tablespoons butter
- ½ cup heavy whipping cream
- ¼ cup parmesan cheese
- ½ cup cheddar cheese
- 1/3 cup chicken broth
- 1 teaspoon dried basil

Nutritional Information

598 Calories;
42g Fat;
6.1g Carbs;
0.5g Fiber;
39g Protein

Directions

In a large pan on medium heat add the vegetable oil.

Cut the pork loin into 2-inch thick medallion. Season with salt and pepper.

Cook the medallion for 3-5 minutes per side or until golden brown. Remove the medallions from the pan and set aside.

In a large skillet add the butter and chopped garlic and cook for 1 minute.

Stir in the heavy whipped cream, chicken broth, parmesan cheese, and cheddar cheese in the skillet. Stir well to combine.

Season with salt, pepper and basil. Simmer for 3-4 minutes or until gets thick.

Place the medallions to the pan and simmer for another 1 minute. Serve warm and enjoy!

Pork Steaks with Spicy Asparagus

Ingredients

- 2 medium pork steaks
- 1 teaspoon Kosher salt
- 1 teaspoon pepper
- 2 tablespoons vegetable oil
- 2 cups fresh asparagus,
- 1 jalapeno, seeded and minced
- 2 cloves garlic, minced
- 3 tablespoons butter

Nutritional Information

403 Calories;
31.8g Fat;
4g Carbs;
1.6g Fiber;
26g Protein

Directions

In a medium skillet put the butter and the minced garlic. Stir well.

Add the fresh asparagus and jalapeno pepper. Cook around 2-3 minutes or until the asparagus is tender. Set aside.

Heat the vegetable oil in a large pan and fry the pork steaks around 5-6 minutes per side or until they are ready. Season with salt and pepper.

Serve the pork steaks along with the spicy asparagus. Enjoy!

Saucy Pork with Tomato Sauce

(Ready in about 20 minutes | Servings 4)

Ingredients

- 4 pork loin chops, boneless
- 2 cloves garlic, minced
- 1 small yellow onion, chopped
- 1 teaspoon paprika
- 2 tablespoons vegetable oil
- 3 large tomatoes, chopped
- ½ teaspoon cilantro
- 2 tablespoons tomato sauce
- 1 small red onion, chopped
- salt and pepper, to taste
- 1 shallot, sliced

Nutritional Information

458 Calories;
26.9g Fat;
7.3g Carbs;
3g Fiber;
42.2g Protein

Directions

Heat a large pan with 1 tablespoon vegetable oil and place the pork chops. Fry for 2-3 minutes per side or until golden brown. Set aside on a plate.

In a large skillet, add the remaining vegetable oil and minced garlic. Saute for 1-2 minutes and add the yellow onion, red onion, and shallot.

Cook for 2-3 minutes and stir in the chopped tomatoes and tomato sauce.

Season with salt, pepper, paprika, and cilantro. Simmer for 5-6 minutes or until the mix is thick.

Place the pork chops in the skillet and cook for 1 minute more. Serve warm and enjoy!

Special Pork Tenderloin with Zucchini

Ingredients

- ½ lb pork tenderloin
- 1/3 cup fresh oregano, chopped
- 3 medium zucchini, sliced into half-moon shapes
- 3 garlic cloves, minced
- 3 tablespoons white wine
- 1 medium onion, chopped
- 1 teaspoon chili pepper
- 1 teaspoon salt
- 1 teaspoon pepper
- 2 tablespoons butter
- 3 tablespoons vegetable broth
- 2 tablespoons vegetable oil

Nutritional Information

434 Calories;
29.3g Fat;
7.1g Carbs;
1.8g Fiber;
32.2g Protein

Directions

Slice the pork into cubes and season with salt and pepper.

Melt the butter in a preheated medium pan on medium heat. Add the pork cubes and cook 3-4 minutes per side or until browned. Set aside.

In a large saucepan add the vegetable oil, garlic, and onion. Saute for 2 minutes. Then stir in the zucchini and cook for 3 minutes more.

Season with salt, pepper, oregano, and chili pepper. Add the white wine and vegetable broth. Stir well and cook for 1-2 minutes.

Serve the pork cubes topped with the zucchini sauce.

Sausage Skillet with Zucchini

(Ready in about 30 min | Servings 6)

Ingredients

- 6 sausages links
- 1 large zucchini, sliced
- 2 garlic cloves, minced
- 1 medium onion, chopped
- 1/3 cup olive oil
- salt and pepper, to taste
- 1 teaspoon dried oregano
- 1 teaspoon dried basil
- 1 cup cherry tomatoes, cut into halves

Nutritional Information

253 Calories;
19.2g Fat;
6.1g Carbs;
1.2g Fiber;
14.7g Protein

Directions

In a large skillet over medium heat, place the sausages and fry until browned. Set aside.

Add the olive oil, minced garlic and chopped onion to the skillet. Cook for 2-3 minutes.

Add in the sliced zucchini and stir well. Cook for 6-7 minutes. Season with salt, pepper, basil and oregano.

Add the cherry tomatoes and cook until soft. Place the sausages back to the skillet and cook for another 2-3 minutes until hot.

Serve immediately. Bon appetite!

BEEF

Marinated Beef Bites

Ingredients

- 2 tablespoons vegetable oil
- 1 lb tenderloin steak, cut into 2-inch cubes
- 1 teaspoon paprika
- ¼ teaspoon salt
- ¼ teaspoon cayenne pepper
- 1 teaspoon garlic powder
- 2 scallions, diced
- ½ teaspoon dried basil
- 1 tablespoon fresh parsley, diced
- 1/2 cup soy sauce

Nutritional Information

441 Calories;
33.6g Fat;
7.5g Carbs;
1.2g Fiber;
25g Protein

Directions

In a large bowl mix the soy sauce, dried basil, garlic powder, cayenne pepper, salt, and paprika. Then soak the beef cubes in the marinade for 30 minutes.

Heat the vegetable oil in a large skillet. Remove the beef cubes from the marinade and add them to the skillet.

Cook for 4 minutes or until golden brown add the diced scallions. Stir occasionally and cook for 2 more minutes.

Sprinkle with fresh parsley and serve.

Beef Flank with Tomato-Pepper Sauce

(Ready in about 30 min | Servings 3)

Ingredients

- 1 lb. flank steak
- 2 red peppers, sliced
- 2 cloves garlic, minced
- 1 teaspoon paprika
- ½ teaspoon cumin
- 2 tablespoons olive oil
- 3 large tomatoes, chopped
- ½ teaspoon cilantro
- 1 red onion, chopped
- salt and pepper, to taste
- 1 jalapeno pepper, chopped optional

Nutritional Information

338 Calories;
17.4g Fat;
6.2g Carbs;
3g Fiber;
34.8g Protein

Directions

Cut the flank steak into ¼- inch thick pieces. Set aside.

In a large skillet add the olive oil, minced garlic and chopped red onion. Fry for 2-3 minutes.

Add the sliced red peppers and cook for 4-5 minutes. Then place the flank steak pieces in the skillet.

Season with salt, pepper, paprika, cumin and cilantro. Cook until brown. Add the chopped tomatoes and cook for 15 minutes.

Serve immediately and garnish with chopped jalapeno pepper (optional).

Stir-Fry Delight with Cabbage

Ingredients

- 1 lb ground beef
- 2 tablespoons olive oil
- 1 scallion, chopped
- 2 cloves garlic, sliced
- 2 cups green cabbage, shredded
- salt and pepper, to taste
- 1 teaspoon red pepper
- 1 teaspoon basil
- 1/2 cup vegetable broth
- 11/3 tablespoon white wine vinegar
- 1 tablespoon sriracha

Nutritional Information

391 Calories;
26.1g Fat;
6.5g Carbs;
1.8g Fiber;
30g Protein

Directions

In a large saucepan heat the olive oil over medium heat. Add the garlic and ground beef to the pan and cook for 4-5 minutes.

Then add the shredded cabbage and stir well. Season with salt, pepper, red pepper and basil.

Stir in the green onion, vegetable broth, and white wine vinegar. Cook for 12-13 minutes or until the cabbage is fully wilted.

Drizzle with the sriracha and serve.

Phenomenal Beef Steaks with Fried Onion

(Ready in about 20 minutes| Servings 2)

Ingredients

- 2 beef sirloin steaks
- 1 teaspoon onion powder
- 1 teaspoon dried oregano
- 1/2 teaspoon salt
- 1 teaspoon dried parsley
- 2 yellow onions, sliced into circles
- 1/3 teaspoon pepper
- 1 teaspoon garlic powder
- 2 tablespoons olive oil
- 1 ½ tablespoon butter

Nutritional Information

530 Calories;
35g Fat;
3.1g Carbs;
0.7g Fiber;
49.9g Protein

Directions

Preheat the olive oil in a medium skillet over medium heat.

Add the onions and cook for 7-8 minutes or until the onions are soft. Stir constantly.

Season with salt and pepper. Remove to a large dish and tent with foil.

Season the beef steaks with salt, pepper, onion powder, dried oregano, dried parsley, and garlic powder.

In a medium pan, preheat the butter. Then add the beef steaks to the pan and fry for 2-3 minutes per side or to the desired doneness.

Serve the sirloin steaks and top with the fried onion.

Quick Beef with Broccoli

Ingredients

- 2 tablespoons butter
- 5 cups broccoli florets
- 1 lb. ground beef
- salt and pepper, to taste
- 1 yellow onion, chopped
- 2 garlic cloves, minced
- ½ teaspoon dried thyme
- 1 teaspoon dried basil
- 2 tablespoons sesame oil

Nutritional Information

402 Calories;
27.8g Fat;
4g Carbs;
2.1g Fiber;
32.3g Protein

Directions

In a large skillet melt the butter. Add the broccoli florets, onion and garlic. Fry for 6-7 minutes. Season with salt, pepper and basil. Set aside.

In another skillet heat the sesame oil.

Add the ground beef and season with salt, pepper and thyme. Cook until it reaches your desired level of doneness.

Serve the beef warm with the broccoli on the side.

Best Beef Chops with Peppers

(Ready in about 20 minutes| Servings 3)

Ingredients

- 1 lb. flank steak, cut into thin strips
- salt and pepper, to taste
- 1 large red pepper, cored and seeded
- 2 cloves garlic, minced
- 1 large green pepper, cored and seeded
- 2 tablespoons vegetable oil
- 2 tablespoons soy sauce
- 1 large yellow pepper, cored and seeded
- 2 teaspoons fresh thyme
- 1/2 cup vegetable broth
- 2 teaspoons sesame seeds

Nutritional Information

351 Calories;
19.7g Fat;
6.8g Carbs;
1.4g Fiber;
34.5g Protein

Directions

Slice the green, red and yellow peppers into thin strips.

Heat 1 tablespoon of the vegetable oil in a large skillet over high heat.

Season the flank steak with salt and pepper.

Place the flank strips in the skillet and cook for 2-3 minutes or until lightly brown. Transfer to a plate and set aside.

In the same skillet add the remaining vegetable oil and garlic. Fry the garlic for 40 sec and stir in the red, green and yellow peppers.

Cook the peppers for 3-4 minutes and add the flank steak back to the saucepan.

Stir in the vegetable broth and soy sauce. Simmer for 1-2 minutes or until the mixture get thick.

Sprinkle with fresh thyme and sesame seeds, then serve. Bon appetite!

Classic Ground Beef with Spinach

(Ready in about 20 minutes | Servings 4)

Ingredients

- 1 lb ground beef
- 2 tablespoons vegetable oil
- 1 teaspoon pepper
- 1 large onion, sliced
- 1 teaspoon dried thyme
- 2 garlic cloves, minced
- 5 cups fresh baby spinach, washed and chopped
- 1 teaspoon Kosher salt
- 1 teaspoon dried oregano
- ½ cup vegetable broth
- ½ cup parmesan cheese, grated
- ¼ cup sour cream

Nutritional Information

499 Calories;
31.3g Fat;
7.1g Carbs;
5.4g Fiber;
40.5g Protein

Directions

Heat the vegetable oil in a preheated medium saucepan on medium heat.

Add the onion and cook for 1-2 minutes until translucent. Stir in the ground beef and season with salt, pepper, thyme and oregano.

Cook until the meat reaches a light brown color. Then add the garlic and spinach to the saucepan. Mix well and cook the spinach until it gets wilted.

Stir in the vegetable broth and cream cheese and cook for 6-7 minutes or until the sauce gets thick. Sprinkle with parmesan and serve. Enjoy!

Flavorful Beef Zoodles

(Ready in about 30 min | Servings 3)

Ingredients

- 3/4 lb. beef flank steak, sliced into 1-inch strips
- 2 medium zucchini, spiralized
- 2 medium carrots, spiralized
- 2 tablespoons coconut oil
- 1/3 teaspoon salt
- 1/3 teaspoon pepper
- 1 teaspoon red pepper flakes
- ¼ cup fresh cilantro, chopped

For the sauce
- 2 tablespoons soy sauce
- 2 cloves garlic, minced
- 2 tablespoons lemon juice

Nutritional Information

296 Calories;
16.9g Fat;
5.3g Carbs;
1.8g Fiber;
26.3g Protein

Directions

In a small bowl prepare the sauce by mixing the minced garlic, soy sauce and lemon juice. Set aside.

In a large skillet add the coconut oil and sliced flank steak.

Cook until the beef is brown and then add the spiralized carrots and zucchini. Then season with salt, pepper and red pepper flakes.

Stir in the prepared sauce and cook for 3-4 minutes. Sprinkle with fresh cilantro and serve!

Flank Steak with Fresh Parsley Pesto

(Ready in about 1 hour and 10 minutes| Servings 4)

Ingredients

- 1 lb flank steak
- 1 teaspoon paprika
- 1 teaspoon dried oregano
- 1/3 cup soy sauce
- 2 tablespoons fresh parsley
- 1 teaspoon red pepper
- 1 teaspoon garlic powder
- 2 tablespoons olive oil
- 1 teaspoon onion powder
- 1/2 teaspoon salt
- ½ teaspoon pepper

For the Parsley Pesto
- 1/3 cup pine nuts
- 2 cups fresh parsley
- 3 cloves garlic, minced
- ½ teaspoon salt
- 1/3 cup olive oil
- ½ teaspoon pepper
- 1/3 cup parmesan cheese
- 2 tablespoons fresh lemon juice

Nutritional Information

571 Calories;
32g Fat;
7.8g Carbs;
2.6g Fiber;
33g Protein

Directions

In a large bowl mix the soy sauce, paprika, olive oil, salt, pepper, dried oregano, red pepper, fresh parsley, garlic powder, and onion powder.

Pour all the ingredients from the bowl in a large plastic bag. Then place the flank steak in the plastic bag and shake well.

Let it marinate in the refrigerator for 40 minutes. Meanwhile, preheat the grill on medium heat.

Place the marinated flank steak on the grill and grill for 5-6 minutes on each side (for medium doneness).

When the steak is ready, leave to rest for 7-8 minutes and slice into thin slices. Set aside.

Meanwhile put the pine nuts, fresh parsley, minced garlic, salt, oil, pepper, parmesan cheese and fresh lemon juice in a blender. Blend until smooth.

Serve the flank steak slices with the parsley pesto on the side.

Hot Beef Ribs in the Oven

Ingredients

- 2 lbs beef short ribs
- ½ cup tomato sauce
- 2 tablespoons olive oil
- 1/2 teaspoon onion powder
- 1 teaspoon cayenne pepper
- ½ teaspoon garlic powder
- 1 teaspoon salt
- 1 tablespoon red pepper flakes
- 1 ½ tablespoon Worcestershire sauce

Nutritional Information

474 Calories;
27.3g Fat;
7g Carbs;
2.4g Fiber;
47g Protein

Directions

Remove the thin membrane that is covering the back of the rack.

Preheat the oven to 350F and place the ribs in a large baking tray.

In a medium bowl combine the tomato sauce, onion powder, cayenne pepper, olive oil, garlic powder, red pepper flakes, Worcestershire sauce and salt. Mix well.

Rub the mixture all over the ribs on both sides. Cover the baking tray with foil and bake for 1 hour.

Leave to cool for 7-8 minutes and serve. Bon appetite!

Cabbage Stir-Fry with Beef

Ingredients

- 2 garlic cloves, minced
- 2 scallions, chopped
- 1 tablespoon white wine vinegar
- 2 ½ cups green cabbage, shredded
- 1 medium yellow onion, chopped
- 1 lbs. ground beef
- 1 teaspoon dried rosemary
- ½ teaspoon dried basil
- salt and pepper, to taste
- 3 tablespoons butter

Nutritional Information

493 Calories;
40g Fat;
6.5g Carbs;
2.8g Fiber;
19.2g Protein

Directions

Melt two tablespoons of butter in a large frying pan. Add the shredded cabbage and cook until soft.

Season with salt, pepper and add the vinegar. Stir well and cook for 3-4 minutes. Set aside.

Heat the rest of the butter in another frying pan. Add the minced garlic and chopped yellow onion. Cook for 2-3 minutes and add the ground beef.

Season with salt, pepper, dried basil and rosemary. Fry until the meat is thoroughly cooked.

Lower the heat and add the chopped scallions and fried cabbage. Stir until everything is hot and serve. Enjoy!

Juicy Stir-Fry Beef with Fresh Asparagus

Ingredients

- 1 lb sirloin steaks, cut into thin strips
- 1 teaspoon Kosher salt
- 1 teaspoon pepper
- 2 tablespoons canola oil
- 1 lbs fresh asparagus, trimmed and cut into 2-inch pieces
- 2 cloves garlic, sliced
- 2 teaspoons lemon juice
- 3 tablespoons butter
- ½ teaspoon red pepper

Nutritional Information

510 Calories;
34.1g Fat;
7.2g Carbs;
3.4g Fiber;
37g Protein

Directions

In a medium skillet put the butter and the minced garlic. Cook for 30 sec.

Then add the fresh asparagus. Cook for 2-3 minutes or until the asparagus get tender.

Season with salt and pepper. Drizzle with the lemon juice and set aside.

Heat the canola oil in a large pan and fry the beef strips for 4-5 minutes per side or until they are ready. Season with salt, pepper and red pepper.

Serve the beef strips immediately with the asparagus.

Magically Delicious Beef Meatballs with Yogurt Dip

(Ready in about 30 minutes| Servings 6)

Ingredients

- 2 lbs ground beef
- 2 tablespoons Parmesan cheese, grated
- 1 egg
- 2 teaspoons fresh thyme
- 1/2 teaspoon salt
- 2 teaspoons garlic powder
- 1 teaspoon oregano
- 1 teaspoon pepper
- 2 teaspoons fresh cilantro
- 2 tablespoons cold water
- 2 tablespoons butter

For the Yogurt Dip
- 1 1/2 cup yogurt
- 1 ½ tablespoon lemon juice
- 1 ½ chopped garlic
- 1 teaspoon cilantro
- 1 teaspoon mint leaves, chopped

Nutritional Information

454 Calories;
30.3g Fat;
2g Carbs;
0.3g Fiber;
40.5g Protein

Directions

Preheat the oven to 400 degrees F.

In a large bowl mix the ground beef, parmesan cheese, egg, fresh thyme, salt, garlic powder, oregano, pepper, fresh cilantro, and cold water.

Mix well with your hands and roll the mixture into medium balls.

Place the meatballs on a baking tray lined with baking sheet.

Bake for 12 minutes then flip for another 10 minutes to the other side or until golden brown. Set aside.

Meanwhile mix the yogurt, lemon juice, garlic, cilantro and mint in a medium bowl. Stir well.

Serve the meatballs with the sauce and enjoy!

Stuffed Zucchini with Beef

(Ready in about 45 minutes | Servings 2)

Ingredients

- 2 zucchinis
- 1/2 cup tomato puree
- 2 cloves garlic, minced
- 1 small yellow onion, finely chopped
- ½ cup Cheddar Cheese, shredded
- 2 tablespoons canola oil
- 1 red pepper, diced
- ½ teaspoon oregano
- ½ teaspoon paprika
- fresh basil leaves, for garnish
- salt and pepper, to taste

Nutritional Information

257 Calories;
15.3g Fat;
8g Carbs;
3.8 Fiber;
4g Protein

Directions

Preheat the oven to 400 degrees F.

Cut the zucchini into halves, take a spoon and scoop out the flesh of the zucchini halves, but leave some at the bottom.

Dice the zucchini flesh into small pieces. Set aside.

Season the zucchini with salt and pepper, place them on a baking tray covered with baking sheet.

In a medium skillet preheat the canola oil.

Add the minced garlic, chopped carrot, diced zucchini flesh, diced red pepper, finely chopped yellow and red onion. Cook until soft.

Season with oregano, paprika, salt, and pepper. Stir well.

Add the tomato sauce and cook for 7 minutes.

Then fill the zucchini with the sauce and top with the shredded cheddar cheese.

Bake for 20 minutes or until golden brown. Then serve and garnish with fresh basil leaves.

Delicious Beef Chuck with Mushroom Sauce

Ingredients

- 1 large onion, diced
- 3 tablespoons olive oil
- 2 cloves garlic, minced
- 1 ½ cup beef broth
- salt and pepper, to taste
- ½ teaspoon dried thyme
- 2 cups mushrooms, cut into ½ inch pieces
- 2 lbs. beef chuck, thinly sliced
- ½ teaspoon tarragon
- 2 tablespoons fresh dill, finely chopped
- 1 cup heavy cream

Nutritional Information

457 Calories;
28g Fat;
7g Carbs;
1.8g Fiber;
40.3g Protein

Directions

Place a large skillet over high heat. Add the olive oil, minced garlic, mushrooms and diced onion. Sauté for 3-4 minutes.

Season with salt, pepper, dried thyme and tarragon. Cook until golden brown.

Pour in the beef broth and simmer for 45 minutes. Remove from heat and add the heavy cream. Stir well.

Serve immediately and garnish with fresh dill. Bon appetite!

FISH & SEAFOOD

Easy-Cheesy White Fish

Ingredients

- 2 tablespoons parmesan cheese, shredded
- 4 fillets white fish
- salt and pepper, to taste
- 2 tablespoons butter, melted
- 2 tablespoons gouda, shredded
- 5 tablespoons milk
- 1 teaspoon mustard
- 2 tablespoons cheddar, shredded
- 1 teaspoon Worcestershire sauce

Nutritional Information

493 Calories;
36g Fat;
3.4g Carbs;
0.3 Fiber;
35.9g Protein

Directions

Preheat the oven to 350F.

Lightly grease a large baking dish with the melted butter. Place the white fish fillets and season with salt and pepper.

In a small bowl mix the cheddar, parmesan and gouda cheese. Then pour the cheese mixture over the fillets.

In another bowl mix the milk, mustard and Worcestershire sauce. Pour over the fish fillets as well.

Bake for 20 minutes or until the fish is cooked through. Serve immediately and enjoy!

Diavolo Shrimp with Tomato Sauce

(Ready in about 20 minutes | Servings 4)

Ingredients

- 3 large tomatoes, chopped
- 4 cloves garlic, minced
- 1 large yellow onion, chopped
- 3 tablespoons fresh parsley, chopped
- 1 ½ lb medium shrimps, peeled and deveined
- 3 tablespoons olive oil
- 2 tablespoons butter
- 1/2 teaspoon pepper
- 1 teaspoon Red pepper flakes
- Kosher salt, to taste
- 1 teaspoon dried rosemary

Nutritional Information

313 Calories;
18g Fat;
8g Carbs;
2.8 Fiber;
25.6g Protein

Directions

Heat the butter in a large pan. Then add the shrimps and cook for 3-4 minutes. Set aside.

In a large skillet add the garlic and onion. Saute for 2 minutes. Stir in the chopped tomatoes and cook for 8-9 minutes or until it has slightly thickened.

Season with Kosher salt, pepper, red pepper flakes, and dried rosemary.

Return the shrimps to the skillet and cook for 1-2 minutes more. Sprinkle with fresh parsley and serve.

Avocado Salad with Shrimp

(Ready in about 10 min | Servings 4)

Ingredients

- 2 tomatoes, sliced into cubes
- 2 medium avocados, cut into large pieces
- 3 tablespoons red onion, diced
- ½ large lettuce, chopped
- 2 lbs. shrimp, peeled and deveined

For the Lime Vinaigrette Dressing

- 2 cloves garlic, minced
- 1 ½ teaspoon Dijon mustard
- 1/3 cup extra virgin olive oil
- salt and pepper to taste
- 1/3 cup lime juice

Nutritional Information

377 Calories;
17.6g Fat;
7g Carbs;
8g Fiber;
43.5g Protein

Directions

Add the peeled and deveined shrimp and 2 quarts of water to a cooking pot and print to a boil, lower the heat and let them simmer for 1-2 minutes until the shrimp is pink. Set aside and let them cool.

Next add the chopped lettuce in a large bowl. Then add the avocado, tomatoes, shrimp and red onion.

In a small bowl whisk together the Dijon mustard, garlic, olive oil and lime juice. Mix well.

Pour the lime vinaigrette dressing over the salad and serve.

Veggie Finnish Salmon Soup

(Ready in about 25 minutes | Servings 4)

Ingredients

- 1 lb salmon fillet, skinned and cut into cubes
- 5 cups vegetable broth
- 1 large onion, chopped
- 1 cup heavy cream
- 2 small carrots, chopped
- salt and pepper, to taste
- 1 celery, chopped
- 1 teaspoon dried basil
- 1 teaspoon thyme
- 3 tablespoons butter
- ½ cup fresh parsley, diced
- 1 cup fresh spinach, rinsed and trimmed
- ½ cup frozen corn

Nutritional Information

329 Calories;
21.3g Fat;
7g Carbs;
1.8 Fiber;
26g Protein

Directions

Heat the butter in a large pot. Then add the onion, corn, carrots, celery, and vegetable broth.

Boil for 10 minutes and stir in the salmon cubes and spinach.

Season with salt, pepper, dried basil and thyme. Continue to boil for 5-6 minutes more.

Add the heavy cream and boil for another 2-3minutes.

Sprinkle with fresh parsley and serve. Bon appetite!

Fried Salmon with Asparagus

(Ready in about 25 minutes | Servings 3)

Ingredients

- 1 cup green asparagus, trimmed
- 2 cloves garlic, sliced
- sea salt and pepper, to taste
- 1 lb salmon fillet, cut into pieces
- 2 tablespoons salted butter
- 2 tablespoons avocado oil
- lemon wedges, optional

Nutritional Information

381 Calories;
25g Fat;
4.9g Carbs;
1.3 Fiber;
32.6g Protein

Directions

In a medium saucepan heat the avocado oil. Add the asparagus and garlic. Cook for 5-6 minutes. Season with sea salt and pepper. Set aside.

Heat the salted butter in a large skillet. Place the salmon pieces in the skillet.

Season with sea salt and pepper. Cook for 3-4 minutes per side or until cooked through.

Serve hot with fresh lemon wedges. Enjoy!

Baked Codfish with Lemon

(Ready in about 25 min | Servings 4)

Ingredients

- 4 fillets codfish
- 1 teaspoon salt
- 1 teaspoon pepper
- 2 tablespoons olive oil
- 2 teaspoons dried basil
- 2 tablespoons melted butter
- 1 teaspoon dried thyme
- 1/3 teaspoon onion powder
- 2 lemons, juiced
- lemon wedges, for garnish

Nutritional Information

308 Calories;
23.6g Fat;
3.9g Carbs;
0.5g Fiber;
21.2g Protein

Directions

Preheat the oven to 400F.

In a medium bowl combine the lemon juice, onion powder, olive oil, dried basil and thyme. Stir well. Season the fillets with salt and pepper.

Top each fillet into the mixture. Then place the fillets into a medium baking dish, greased with melted butter.

Bake the codfish fillets for 15-20 minutes. Serve with fresh lemon wedges. Enjoy!

Colorful Sardines Omelet

(Ready in about 10 minutes | Servings 2)

Ingredients

- 4 eggs
- 1 tablespoon red bell pepper, chopped
- 1 tablespoon yellow bell pepper, chopped
- 1 tablespoon green bell pepper, chopped
- salt and pepper, to taste
- 1 can sardines, drained and cut into small pieces
- 1 ½ tablespoon vegetable oil
- 1 tablespoon cheddar cheese, shredded
- ½ cup cherry tomatoes, cut into halves

Nutritional Information

397 Calories;
30g Fat;
7.9g Carbs;
1.5 Fiber;
22g Protein

Directions

Heat the vegetable oil in a large pan.

Add the chopped green, yellow and red pepper. Saute for 1-2 minutes and add the eggs and sardines.

Season with salt and pepper. Then fry until the egg mixture is almost cooked through.

Add the shredded cheddar cheese and fold the omelet in a half moon shape.

Serve with fresh cherry tomatoes.

Mediterranean Crab Meat Salad

Ingredients

- ½ lb fresh crab meat, sliced
- 1 scallion, sliced
- 1 celery, chopped
- 1/3 cup fresh parsley, chopped
- salt and pepper, to taste
- 4 tablespoons mayonnaise
- ½ tablespoon lemon juice
- ½ tablespoon Dijon mustard

Directions

In a large bowl combine the sliced scallion, celery, and crab meat. Mix well.

Stir in the mayonnaise, chopped parsley and Dijon mustard. Season with salt, pepper and lemon juice.

Refrigerate for 1 hour and serve. Bon appetite!

Nutritional Information

208 Calories;
10.9g Fat;
8g Carbs;
3.8 Fiber;
22.8g Protein

Family Salmon with Kale Pesto

(Ready in about 30 min | Servings 4)

Ingredients

- 2 lbs. salmon fillets
- 3 tablespoons olive oil
- ¾ teaspoon sea salt
- lemon pepper to taste

Kale Pesto
- 1/3 cup walnuts
- ½ teaspoon black pepper
- 2 tablespoons olive oil
- 2 garlic cloves
- 1 cup kale, chopped
- 2 tablespoons lemon juice
- 1 teaspoon salt

Nutritional Information

508 Calories;
29.8g Fat;
3.4g Carbs;
1.1g Fiber;
54.5g Protein

Directions

Put the chopped kale, garlic, olive oil, walnuts and lemon juice in a blender. Blend until smooth. Season with salt and pepper. Set aside.

Season the salmon fillets with the sea salt and lemon pepper. Brush with olive oil.

Preheat a grill pan on medium heat. Place the salmon fillets on the preheated grill pan for 5 to 7 minutes per side or until the fish is done.

Serve the salmon fillets with the kale pesto. Bon appetite!

Pan-Fried Monkfish Medallions with Lemon Sauce

(Ready in about 20min | Servings 2)

Ingredients

- 1 ½ lbs. monkfish, cut into medallions
- salt and pepper, to taste
- 2 tablespoons olive oil
- lemon wedges, for serving

For the lemon sauce
- 3 tablespoons butter, melted
- ½ lemon, juiced
- salt and pepper, to taste
- 1 tablespoon Dijon mustard

Nutritional Information

328 Calories;
17.5g Fat;
3.9g Carbs;
0.5g Fiber;
37.3g Protein

Directions

Season the monkfish with salt and pepper.

Place a frying pan over a medium heat and add the olive oil. Add the monkfish medallions to the pan and cook on both sides until golden brown. Set aside.

In a small bowl mix the melted butter, lemon juice, Dijon mustard, salt and pepper. Stir well.

Serve the monkfish medallions with the lemon wedges and drizzle with the lemon sauce.

Quick Spinach Salad with Shrimps

Ingredients

- 2 cups spinach, chopped
- 2 stalks celery, finely diced
- 1 green onion, diced
- 1 lb boiled shrimp, peeled and deveined
- 1/3 cup blue cheese, crumbled
- 2 tablespoons fresh parsley, chopped
- 1/4 cup extra virgin olive oil
- 1/3 teaspoon salt
- 1/3 cup lemon juice
- 1 tablespoon white wine vinegar

Directions

In a large bowl mix the spinach, diced celery and chopped green onion. Stir.

Add the shrimps and blue cheese. Combine well. Season with salt, lemon juice, olive oil and white wine vinegar.

Serve with fresh parsley. Enjoy!

Nutritional Information

288 Calories;
14.4g Fat;
3.4g Carbs;
3.8 Fiber;
35g Protein

Fried Sardines with Lemon Sauce

(Ready in about 15 minutes | Servings 2)

Ingredients

- 8 fresh sardines, gutted and cleaned
- 4 tablespoons vegetable oil
- ½ teaspoon oregano
- 2 tablespoons lemon juice
- 4 tablespoons unsalted butter
- salt and pepper, to taste
- lemon wedges, for serving

Nutritional Information

493 Calories;
48g Fat;
5g Carbs;
0.8 Fiber;
15g Protein

Directions

Melt the unsalted butter in a small skillet for 3 minutes.

Then pour the butter in a small bowl and add the lemon juice, salt, and pepper. Stir well. Set aside.

Heat the vegetable oil in a large saucepan then add the sardines and season with salt, pepper and oregano. Fry for 2-3 minutes per side.

Drain the sardines on a paper towel and transfer to a plate.

Drizzle with the sauce and garnish with lemon wedges.

Simple Sole Fillet with Butter Sauce

Ingredients

- 1 lb petrale sole fillets
- 3 tablespoons unsalted butter
- 1 teaspoon thyme
- 2 tablespoons shallot, minced
- 2 tablespoons lime juice
- 2 tablespoons avocado oil
- 1/3 cup white wine
- salt and pepper, to taste
- 1/3 cup fresh parsley, chopped

Nutritional Information

207 Calories;
15g Fat;
3.1g Carbs;
0.6 Fiber;
16g Protein

Directions

Heat the avocado oil in a large saucepan.

Season the sole fillets with salt and pepper. Fry for 2-3 minutes per side and set aside.

In a skillet melt the butter. Then add the minced shallots and fry for 2 minutes.

Stir in the white wine and lime juice. Season with salt, pepper and thyme. Stir well and cook for 3 minutes.

Drizzle the sauce over the sole filets and sprinkle with fresh parsley. Enjoy!

Teriyaki Shrimp Skewers

(Ready in about 1 hour | Servings 6)

Ingredients

- 2 lbs. medium shrimp, peeled and deveined
- 3 cloves garlic, minced
- ½ teaspoon salt
- ½ teaspoon pepper
- 12 bamboo skewers
- 1 tablespoon honey
- 2 tablespoons lemon juice
- 1/3 cup olive oil
- ½ teaspoon lime zest
- lemon wedges for serving
- 1/2 tablespoon cilantro, chopped
- ½ cup teriyaki sauce

Nutritional Information

251 Calories;
13.5g Fat;
7g Carbs;
0.2g Fiber;
22.3g Protein

Directions

Soak the bamboo skewers in water for 20 minutes.

In a large bowl combine the minced garlic, honey, lemon juice, olive oil, lime zest and teriyaki sauce. Season with salt, pepper and cilantro. Mix well.

Add the shrimp to the bowl and marinate for 20 minutes in the refrigerator.

Preheat the grill over medium heat.

Thread the shrimp onto skewers, about 3 per stick. Place the shrimp skewers on the grill. Cook for 2-3 minutes per side.

Serve with lemon wedges. Bon appetite!

Spicy Sushi Roll with Cucumber and Tuna

Ingredients

- 1 large cucumber
- 1 can tuna, drained
- 1/3 cup cream cheese
- salt and pepper, to taste
- ½ teaspoon chili powder
- 1 jalapeno, thinly sliced
- 1 ½ teaspoon sesame seeds

Nutritional Information

242 Calories;
13.9g Fat;
7.9g Carbs;
3 Fiber;
21.2g Protein

Directions

Cut the cucumber into thin slices with a vegetable peeler.

In a small bowl mix the tuna, cream cheese and chili powder. Season with salt and pepper. Stir well.

Spread a small amount of the tuna mixture onto the cucumber strips. Then place the jalapeno slices in the end of cucumber strips and roll.

Sprinkle with sesame seeds and serve. Bon appetite!

EGGS & DAIRY

Avocado Boats with Tuna Mayo

Ingredients

- 2 large avocados
- ½ teaspoon salt
- ½ teaspoon pepper
- 10 tablespoons mayonnaise
- 1 cup of canned tuna
- 1 fresh onion, thinly chopped

Nutritional Information

346 Calories;
27g Fat;
8g Carbs;
8g Fiber;
14g Protein

Directions

In a medium bowl mix the mayonnaise and tuna. Season with salt and pepper.

Cut the avocado into halves and remove the pit. Then fill the center with the mayo mixture.

Sprinkle immediately with the fresh onion and serve.

Creamy Broccoli Soup

Ingredients

- 2 cups broccoli, chopped
- 2 tablespoons olive oil
- 1 ½ cup cheddar cheese, shredded
- 1/3 cup whipping cream
- 1 teaspoon garlic powder
- 1 large yellow onion, chopped
- ½ teaspoon salt
- ½ teaspoon pepper
- 5 cups vegetable broth

Nutritional Information

114 Calories;
8g Fat;
7g Carbs;
1.3g Fiber;
2.1g Protein

Directions

In a medium pot add the olive oil. Saute the onion for 1minute or until fragrant.

Add the vegetable broth and broccoli. Season with salt, pepper and garlic powder.

Cook until the broccoli is tender. Then stir in the whipping cream and cheddar cheese.

Boil until it gets thick. Serve hot and enjoy!

Cauliflower Casserole with Cheddar

(Ready in about 35 minutes | Servings 4)

Ingredients

- 1 medium head cauliflower, cut into florets
- 1 cup sour cream
- ½ cup heavy cream
- 2 tablespoons butter
- 3 garlic cloves, minced
- 1 cup cheddar cheese, shredded
- ½ cup parmesan cheese, grated
- ¼ cup green onion, chopped
- salt and pepper, to taste

Nutritional Information

259 Calories;
20.9g Fat;
7g Carbs;
3g Fiber;
8.2g Protein

Directions

In a large stockpot of boiling water add the cauliflower florets. Boil for 3-4 minutes.

Drain the cauliflower and set aside.

In a medium saucepan melt the butter. Add the minced garlic and green onion. Cook for 1 minute.

Whisk in the sour cream and heavy cream. Combine well. Season with salt and pepper.

Add the cheddar and parmesan cheese to the saucepan and cook for 2-3 miniutes.

In a casserole dish add the cauliflower and pour the cheese sauce.

Bake in a preheated oven to 400 F for 30 minutes. Serve hot!

Asparagus with Sauce "Hollandaise"

Ingredients

- 1lb. green asparagus
- 3 tablespoons butter
- salt and pepper to taste
-
- For the sauce
- 3 egg yolks
- 2 tablespoons water
- 2 tablespoons olive oil
- juice of 1/2 lemon
- salt and red pepper to taste

Nutritional Information

236 Calories;
21.8g Fat;
6.9g Carbs;
2.5g Fiber;
5.6g Protein

Directions

In a bowl whisk the yolks and add cold water. Stir well.

Melt the butter in a saucepan and pour a thin stream of yolks. Constantly stir. Season with salt, red pepper and lemon juice.

Clean and cut the asparagus 2-3 inches from the base. Grill the asparagus for 1-2 minutes on each side.

Serve the asparagus and top with the sauce! Bon appetite!

Grandma's Cheesy Omelet

(Ready in about 10 minutes | Servings 3)

Ingredients

- 3 eggs
- 1 tablespoon cheddar cheese, shredded
- 1 tablespoon butter
- 1 thick slice ham, chopped
- salt and pepper, to taste
- 1 tablespoon yellow onion, chopped
- 1/3 cup cherry tomatoes, cut in halves

Nutritional Information

450 Calories;
34.9g Fat;
7.6g Carbs;
1.5g Fiber;
24.2g Protein

Directions

In a small bowl whisk the eggs and add the shredded cheddar cheese. Mix well. Season with salt and pepper and set aside.

Melt the butter in a frying pan. Saute the chopped ham and onion for 2-3 minutes. Then add the egg mixture and fry until cooked through.

Serve with fresh cherry tomatoes on top.

Delicious Creamy Spinach

(Ready in about 15 minutes | Servings 3)

Ingredients

- 3 cups fresh spinach leaves
- 3 tablespoons butter
- ½ cup heavy cream
- 2 garlic cloves, minced
- 1 large yellow onion, diced
- 1/3 cup parmesan cheese, grated
- salt and pepper, to taste

Nutritional Information

252 Calories;
22.3g Fat;
8g Carbs;
1.8g Fiber;
6.1g Protein

Directions

In a large skillet heat the butter.

Add the minced garlic and diced onion. Cook for 2-3 minutes.

Place the spinach in the skillet and season with salt and pepper. Stir well and saute for 3-4 minutes. Pour in the heavy cream and grated parmesan cheese.

Cook until spinach thickens. Serve immediately and bon appetite!

Scrambled Eggs with Kale and Mozzarella

(Ready in about 15 min | Servings 3)

Ingredients

- 2 cups kale leaves, coarsely chopped
- 10 large eggs
- 2 teaspoons olive oil
- 1 small onion, finely chopped
- 1 teaspoon salt
- 1 teaspoon pepper
- 2 cloves garlic, minced
- 1 teaspoon oregano
- ½ cup mozzarella cheese, grated

Nutritional Information

260 Calories;
18.2g Fat;
6.6g Carbs;
1.5g Fiber;
16.4g Protein

Directions

In a saucepan add the olive oil, finely chopped onion, minced garlic and kale leaves. Cook for 2-3 minutes and then add the eggs. Stir well.

Add the grated mozzarella cheese to the saucepan and stir until the eggs are ready. Season with salt, pepper and oregano.

Serve immediately and enjoy!

Egg Muffins with Bacon

(Ready in about 20 min | Servings 6)

Ingredients

- 6 large eggs
- ½ cup cooked bacon, chopped
- ½ cup cheddar cheese, shredded
- salt and pepper, to taste
- ½ teaspoon dried basil
- ½ teaspoon dried oregano
- chives for garnish (optional)

Nutritional Information

156 Calories;
12.8g Fat;
3.9g Carbs;
0.5g Fiber;
10g Protein

Directions

Preheat the oven to 350F.

In a medium bowl whisk together the eggs, salt, pepper, dried basil and dried oregano. Mix well. Add the chopped bacon and shredded cheddar cheese. Stir.

Fill each muffin cup with the egg mixture. Bake for 15 minutes or until the eggs are set.

Garnish with chives and serve. Bon appetite!

Creamy Stuffed Spinach Eggs

(Ready in about 30 min | Servings 20)

Ingredients

- 10 eggs
- 1 teaspoon lime juice
- 1 cup spinach
- 1 teaspoon salt
- 1 teaspoon red pepper
- 1 teaspoon pepper
- 1 teaspoon olive oil

Nutritional Information

137 Calories;
10.8g Fat;
1.7g Carbs;
0.1g Fiber;
9.4g Protein

Directions

Put the eggs in a saucepan and cover with water. Boil for 14 minutes.

After the eggs are boiled, drain the hot water. Add cold water to the eggs and leave them to cool for 1-2 minutes.

Peel and cut the eggs into halves. Separate the yolks.

Clean and cut the spinach. Sauté the spinach in a saucepan with olive oil and add the separated yolks. Mix well.

Add the salt, pepper and red pepper to the mixture. Stir until the mixture gets thick and smooth. Then, leave it to cool for a couple of minutes.

Put the egg whites cut-side-up on a serving dish.

With a spoon, take from the mixture and stuff each egg. Drizzle with lime juice. Serve!

Easy Baked Tomatoes with Mozzarella

(Ready in about 15 minutes | Servings 4)

Ingredients

- 1 ½ cup mozzarella cheese, shredded
- 1 teaspoon fresh oregano, chopped
- 4 Heirloom tomatoes, halved horizontally
- 1/3 teaspoon salt
- 1/3 teaspoon pepper
- ½ cup parmesan cheese, grated
- 2 tablespoons olive oil
- 2 tablespoons fresh basil, chopped

Nutritional Information

192 Calories;
10.9g Fat;
7.9g Carbs;
1.9g Fiber;
18.4g Protein

Directions

Preheat the oven to 350F.

In a medium bowl mix the shredded mozzarella cheese, parmesan cheese, fresh oregano, salt and pepper.

In a large baking dish on parchment paper, place the tomatoes. Top each tomato with the prepared cheese mixture.

Drizzle with the olive oil and bake for 10 minutes. Then garnish with fresh basil and serve.

Goat Cheese with Pecan

Ingredients

- 1 lb log goat cheese
- 1/3 cup pecans, chopped
- 3 tablespoons yacon syrup
- 2 teaspoons fresh basil, chopped
- 1 teaspoon fresh chives, chopped

Nutritional Information

296 Calories;
21.9g Fat;
8g Carbs;
0.6g Fiber;
14.2g Protein

Directions

In a small saucepan add the chopped basil, yacon and chives. Cook for 1-2 minutes and set aside.

Finely chop the pecans and transfer them on a large plate. Then roll the goat cheese in the chopped pecans.

Drizzle with the yacon mixture and serve. Enjoy!

Mayo Egg Salad

Ingredients

- 6 eggs, hard-boiled
- 1/3 cup mayonnaise
- 1 ½ teaspoon Dijon mustard
- 1/3 cup green onions, finely sliced
- 1 teaspoon lemon juice
- 1/3 teaspoon salt
- 1 stalk celery, finely chopped
- 1/2 teaspoon curry powder
- 1 tablespoon fresh parsley, chopped

Directions

Peel and chop the eggs into small pieces.

In a medium bowl mix the mayonnaise and Dijon mustard. Add the chopped eggs, green onions, celery and lemon juice. Stir well.

Season with salt and curry powder. Sprinkle with fresh parsley and serve. Bon appetite!

Nutritional Information

263 Calories;
20.9g Fat;
2.9g Carbs;
0.6g Fiber;
15g Protein

Spinach Muffins with Parmesan

Ingredients

- 6 large eggs
- 1/3 teaspoon garlic powder
- salt and pepper, to taste
- ½ teaspoon dried basil
- 1 ½ cup spinach, chopped
- 1 ½ cup parmesan cheese, grated

Nutritional Information

165 Calories;
12.1g Fat;
5.2g Carbs;
0.4g Fiber;
11.2g Protein

Directions

Preheat the oven to 350F.

In a medium bowl whisk together the eggs, salt, pepper and dried basil. Mix well. Stir in the spinach and grated parmesan cheese. Mix well.

Fill each muffin cup with the egg mixture. Then bake for 15 minutes or until the eggs are set.

Sprinkle with more cheese and serve. Enjoy!

Triple Cheese Stuffed Red Peppers

(Ready in about 25 minutes | Servings 4)

Ingredients

- 4 red peppers, cut in half and cleaned
- ½ cup mozzarella cheese, shredded
- ½ cup parmesan cheese, shredded
- 2 tablespoons olive oil
- ½ cup ricotta cheese
- ½ teaspoon dried basil
- ½ teaspoon dried oregano
- salt and pepper, to taste
- 2 tablespoons fresh parsley

Nutritional Information

210 Calories;
14.5g Fat;
8g Carbs;
1.3g Fiber;
12.6g Protein

Directions

Preheat the oven to 350F.

In a small bowl mix together the shredded mozzarella cheese, parmesan cheese and ricotta cheese. Mix. Season with salt, pepper, basil and oregano.

Place the peppers on a baking sheet in a large baking dish. Drizzle with olive oil and fill the peppers with the cheese mixture.

Bake for 15-20 minutes. Sprinkle with fresh parsley and serve. Bon appetite!

Coleslaw with Eggs

Ingredients

- 3 cups cabbage, shredded
- 2 large eggs, boiled
- 1 ½ tablespoon Dijon Mustard
- ½ cup mayonnaise
- ½ teaspoon salt
- ½ teaspoon pepper
- 2 tablespoons fresh parsley, chopped
- 1 teaspoon poppy seeds
- 1 tablespoon white vinegar

Nutritional Information

167 Calories;
13g Fat;
6.8g Carbs;
2.5g Fiber;
6.8g Protein

Directions

In a small bowl prepare dressing by mixing the Dijon mustard, mayonnaise and white vinegar. Set aside.

Peel the eggs and chop them. Then in a large bowl mix the shredded cabbage, chopped parsley and chopped eggs.

Stir in the prepared dressing and combine well. Season with salt, pepper and poppy seeds.

Put in the refrigerator for 1 hour before serving. Serve cold and enjoy!

Yummy Cheesy Balls

(Ready in about 10 minutes | Servings 6)

Ingredients

- 4 tablespoons cheddar cheese, shredded
- ½ cup bacon bits
- 2 teaspoons Dijon mustard
- 1 teaspoon dried parsley
- 1 tablespoon green onion, thinly chopped
- 1 teaspoon dried chives
- 1 ½ cup cream cheese, softened
- ½ teaspoon salt
- ½ teaspoon pepper

Nutritional Information

299 Calories;
24.9g Fat;
5.2g Carbs;
1.1g Fiber;
12.2g Protein

Directions

In a large bowl add the softened cream cheese and Dijon mustard. Mix well.

Stir in the cheddar cheese, bacon bits and green onion. Season with salt, pepper, dried parsley and chives.

With hands make 12 walnut-sized balls.

Place the balls on a wax paper and refrigerate for 1 hour until ready to serve. Enjoy!

DESSERTS

Cocoa Smoothie

(Ready in about 5 minutes | Servings 2)

Ingredients

- 1 cup coconut milk
- 2 tablespoons cocoa powder
- ½ teaspoon vanilla extract
- ½ cup water
- ½ avocado
- ½ teaspoon cinnamon

Nutritional Information

320 Calories;
30.1g Fat;
7.5g Carbs;
4.1g Fiber;
5g Protein

Directions

Add the coconut milk, avocado, cocoa powder, cinnamon, vanilla extract and water in a blender.

Blend until smooth.

Serve immediately and enjoy!

Avocado Ice Pops with Lime

(Ready in about 5 min | Servings 10)

Ingredients

- ¼ cup lime juice
- 3 avocados, ripe, peeled and stone removed
- 2 tablespoons honey
- 1 ½ cup coconut milk
- 3 tablespoons water, if seems thick

Nutritional Information

197 Calories;
17.4g Fat;
7g Carbs;
4.9g Fiber;
2.7g Protein

Directions

Put all of the above ingredients in a blender and mix until it reaches a smooth consistency.

If the mixture seems very thick add a little water.

Pour the mixture into popsicle molds.

Freeze for 5 hours or up to overnight.

Bon appetite!

Blackberry Coconut Treat

(Ready in about 45 min | Servings 8)

Ingredients

- 1 cup fresh blackberries
- 1/2 teaspoon vanilla extract
- 1/2 cup coconut oil, softened
- 2 tablespoons water
- 1 teaspoon vanilla liquid stevia
- ½ tablespoon lemon juice
- Pinch of salt
- 1/2 cup coconut butter, softened

Nutritional Information

238 Calories;
25.4g Fat;
4.2g Carbs;
0.6g Fiber;
1g Protein

Directions

Put all the ingredients in a blender. Blend until smooth and thick.

Line an 8 capacity muffin pan with silicone cupcake liners.

Pour the mixture into each cup, about half-way.

Refrigerate 3-4 hours or freeze for 40 minutes. Enjoy!

Favorite Tiramisu Mousse

Ingredients

- 1 ½ cup mascarpone cheese
- 2 tablespoons erythritol
- ½ cup heavy cream
- cocoa powder, for dusting
- 1/3 cup espresso
- 1/3 cup dark rum
- 1 teaspoon vanilla

Nutritional Information

314 Calories;
21g Fat;
3g Carbs;
0g Fiber;
12g Protein

Directions

In a large bowl add the mascarpone cheese and heavy cream.

With an electronic mixer beat for 3-4 minutes until smooth consistency is reached.

Stir in the erythritol, espresso, dark rum and vanilla. Mix well.

Pour the mixture into serving glasses and dust with the cocoa powder.

Refrigerate for 40 minutes and serve.

No-Bake Cheesecake in a Glass

(Ready in about 45 minutes | Servings 4)

Ingredients

Crust
- 2 tablespoons melted butter
- 1/2 cup almond flour
- ½ tablespoon erythritol

Filling
- ½ teaspoon cinnamon
- ½ teaspoon vanilla extract
- ½ cup Philadelphia cream cheese
- 1/3 cup whipping cream
- 1 ½ tablespoon cocoa powder
- 1/3 cup crème fraiche
- ½ cup fresh blackberries
- mint leaves, for decoration

Nutritional Information

213 Calories;
16.3g Fat;
8g Carbs;
2g Fiber;
4g Protein

Directions

Add the melted butter, almond flour and erythritol in a medium bowl. Mix until well combined.

Press the mixture into four serving glasses and set aside.

In a large bowl add the Philadelphia cream cheese, whipping cream and crème fraiche.

Mix with an immersion blender until the mixture is light and fluffy.

Stir in the vanilla extract, cinnamon and cocoa powder. Mix for 1 minute more.

Spoon from the cheesecake mixture into the serving glasses.

Top with fresh blackberries and mint leaves. Place in the refrigerator for 30 minutes.

Serve and bon appetite!

Pink Strawberry Ice Cream

Ingredients

- 2 ½ cups coconut cream
- 1 cup fresh strawberries
- 1/3 cup Swerve sweetener
- 1 ½ teaspoon vanilla powder
- fresh strawberries (for decoration)

Nutritional Information

412 Calories;
41.5g Fat;
7.4g Carbs;
3.4g Fiber;
4.7g Protein

Directions

Add the coconut cream and fresh strawberries in a blender.

Blend until a smooth consistency is reached.

Add the vanilla powder and swerve. Blend again.

Place the mixture into airtight container and freeze for 7-8 hours.

Before serving decorate with fresh strawberries. Bon appetite!

Coconut Pudding

Ingredients

- 1/3 teaspoon salt
- 3 teaspoon Coconut liquid stevia
- 4 teaspoon gelatin
- 32 oz coconut milk unsweetened, canned
- 2 teaspoon vanilla extract

Optional toppings

- fresh berries
- unsweet coconut flakes

Nutritional Information

300 Calories;
32.4g Fat;
5.1g Carbs;
0g Fiber;
1g Protein

Directions

In a saucepan put the coconut milk over medium heat. Stir constantly until it comes to a boil.

Reduce heat to simmer and add the gelatin. Stir well until the mixture gets thick.

Remove from the heat and stir in the vanilla extract, salt and coconut liquid stevia.

Pour into 6 medium jars. Leave to cool 40 minutes then refrigerate for 3-4 hours.

Serve with fresh berries or unsweet coconut flakes.

No-Bake Coconut Balls

Ingredients

- 3 tablespoons xylitol
- 1 teaspoon vanilla
- 1 teaspoon salt
- 1 ½ cups organic unsweetened shredded coconut
- 3 tablespoons coconut oil

Nutritional Information

177 Calories;
15g Fat;
6.9g Carbs;
1g Fiber;
0.7g Protein

Directions

In a blender combine all the ingredients until the mixture sticks together.

Remove the mixture from the blender and with hands form small balls.

Decorate the balls with some extra shredded coconut.

Leave them in the refrigerator for 20-25 minutes. Bon appetite!

Purple Raspberry Mousse

Ingredients

- 1 teaspoon vanilla extract
- 1 cup fresh raspberries
- 1 ½ cup heavy cream
- 1 tablespoon cocoa powder
- 2 tablespoons brazil nuts, chopped

Nutritional Information

194 Calories;
18.9g Fat;
6g Carbs;
1.5g Fiber;
3.2g Protein

Directions

In a large bowl add the heavy cream, raspberries, vanilla extract and cocoa powder.

Mix with an immersion blender for 3 minutes. Then stir in the chopped brazil nuts and refrigerate for 30 minutes.

Place the mousse into small bowls and serve.

Lemon Delights

Ingredients

- 4 large eggs
- 1 ½ cups lemon juice
- 1/2 cup butter, melted
- 1 1/2 cups almond flour
- Pinch of salt
- 1 ½ cup Swerve sweetener
- 2 tablespoons coconut oil, grease baking pan
- 8 lemon slices

Nutritional Information

136 Calories;
13.5g Fat;
2g Carbs;
0.1g Fiber;
1.7g Protein

Directions

Preheat the oven to 400 °F and rub an 8x8 inch pan with the coconut oil.

Mix 1 cup almond flour, ½ cup melted butter, a pinch of salt and 1 cup Swerve until well combined.

Place the dough into the prepared form and bake until light brown. Set aside.

In a bowl mix ½ cup almond flour,4 eggs, ½ cup Swerve, a pinch of salt and the lemon juice. Mix well.

Pour the mixture onto the cooled crust and bake around 20 minutes or until it is done.

Let it cool at room temperature and place in the refrigerator for a few hours.

Serve with fresh lemon slices. Enjoy!

Made in the USA
Middletown, DE
08 February 2020